Mallorca Living

Concept Paco Asensio

Editor Haike Falkenberg

Art Direction Mireia Casanovas Soley

Text © Gloria Torrens Ferrer 2001

Photographs © Pere Planells 2001

English Translation Harry Paul

German Translation Inken Wolthaus

Editorial Project © Loft Publications S.L. 2001
Domènec 9, 2-2.
08012 Barcelona. Spain
T. 34 93 218 30 99
Fax.: 34 93 237 00 60
loft@loftpublications.com
www.loftpublications.com

Die Deutsche Bibliothek - CIP-Zentrale

Mallorca Living / Gloria Torrens Ferrer. Fotogr. von Pere Planells. - Orig.-Ausg. - Köln : DuMont, 2001
(Monte von DuMont)
ISBN 3-7701-8680-X

Majorca Living / Gloria Torrens Ferrer. Photrogr. Pere Planells.
© 2001DuMont Buchverlag, Köln
(Dumont monte, UK, London)
ISBN 3-7701-7121-7

Originalausgabe
© 2001 DuMont Buchverlag, Köln
Alle Rechte vorbehalten
Druck: Druckerei Appl, Wemding

Printed in Germany

ISBN 3-7701-8680-X

City

Stadt

Country

Land

Sea

Meer

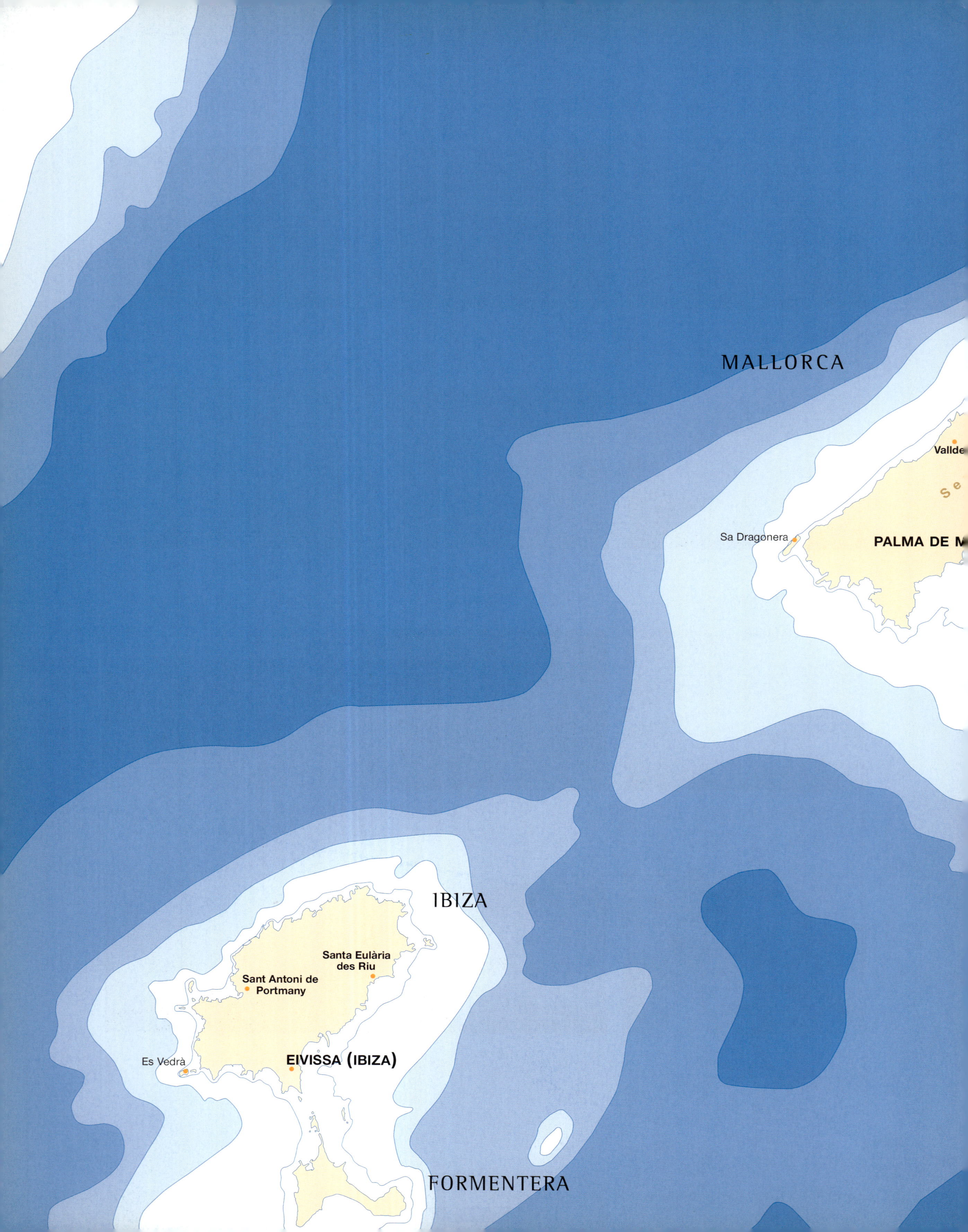
MALLORCA
Valldе
Se
Sa Dragonera
PALMA DE M
IBIZA
Santa Eulària des Riu
Sant Antoni de Portmany
Es Vedrà
EIVISSA (IBIZA)
FORMENTERA

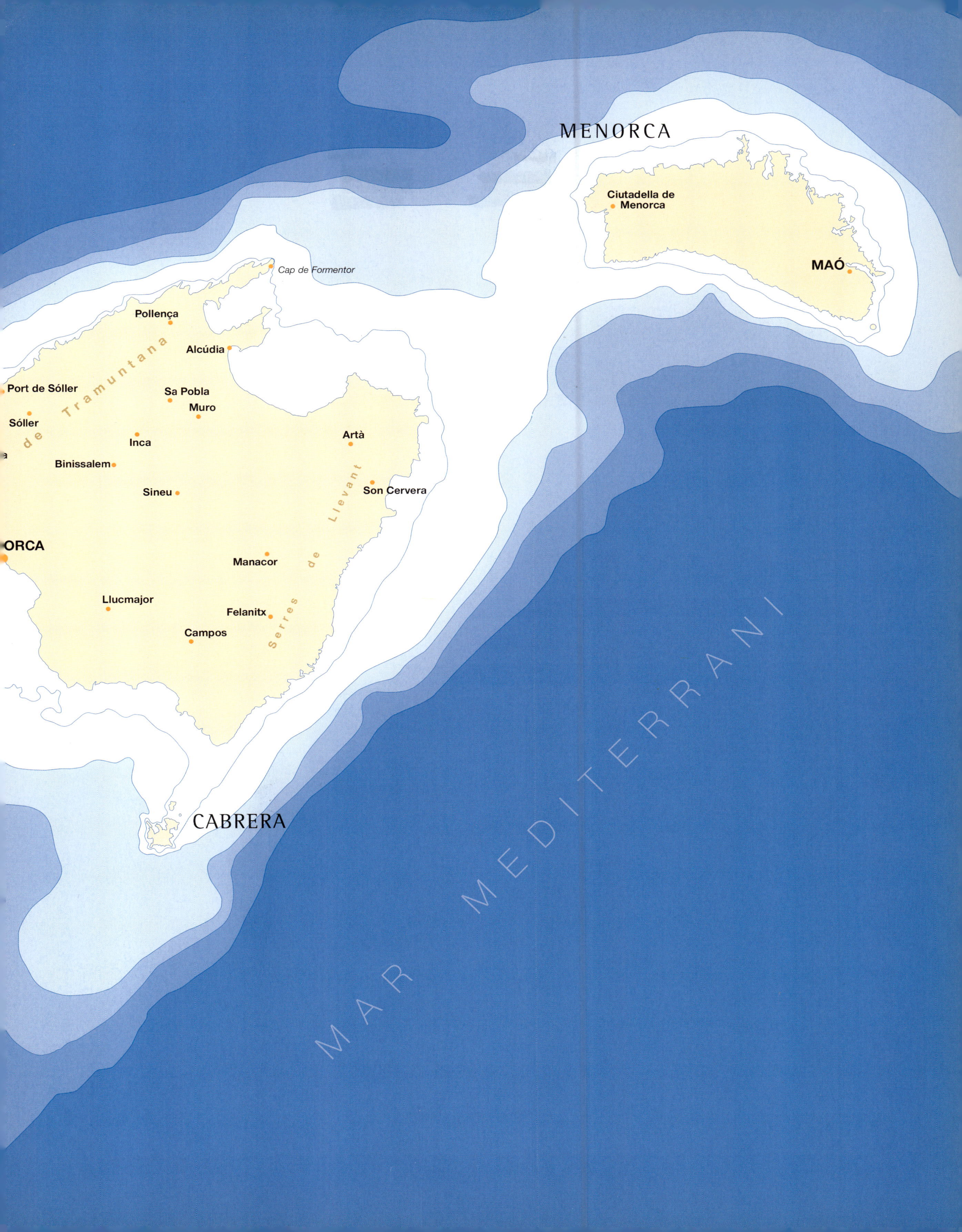
MENORCA
Ciutadella de Menorca
MAÓ
Cap de Formentor
Pollença
Alcúdia
Port de Sóller
Sa Pobla
Muro
Sóller
Inca
Artà
Binissalem
Sineu
Son Cervera
Serres de Llevant
de Tramuntana
ORCA
Manacor
Llucmajor
Felanitx
Campos
CABRERA
MAR MEDITERRANI

Introduction

Whenever you enter into a new world, or come to the landing port of uncharted territory, you must open your eyes and spirit so as to be prepared to perceive all the sensations possible. The objective of this book is to help us do that. Experience teaches us that the more we know about something, the deeper we can get into its roots and obtain more insight. This is the motivation behind the texts and the photos of this book, which delve into the history, the daily customs, the traditions and everyday life of a people whose millenary culture dates back to the origins of Mediterranean civilization.

When looking for a word which would sum up what the Mediterranean life style is about we would have to go for "tranquility". At the opposite end of the spectrum we are aware of the stress and pressure which so obtrusively invade our lives, leaving us without a moment for ourselves. Looking around and trying to let the peacefulness of our surroundings reach into

Einleitung

Betritt man eine neue Welt oder unerforschtes Land, muss man Augen und Sinne öffnen, um alle möglichen Eindrücke aufnehmen zu können, die sich einem bieten. Dies möglich zu machen, ist das Ziel dieses Buches. Die Erfahrung lehrt uns, dass je umfassender unser Wissen von einer Sache ist, desto tiefer dringen wir zu den Wurzeln vor und vervollständigen somit unser Bild der Dinge. In dieser Absicht wagt sich dieses Werk – in Worten und Bildern – in die historischen Ursprünge, das Alltagsleben, die Sitten und Gebräuche eines Volkes mit jahrtausendealter Kultur mediterraner Herkunft vor.

Versucht man, in einem Begriff zusammen zu fassen, was der mediterrane Lebensstil ist, macht sich spontan ein erster Gedanke breit: Ruhe. Die anderen Extreme sind der Druck und Stress eines hektischen Lebens, in dem die Besinnung auf sich selbst keinen Platz findet. Es tut Not, sich umzuschauen und die friedliche Ausstrahlung der Umgebung auf sich wir-

us is time well spent. An idyllic landscape can make us forget any predicament, helping us to see any worry, setback or suffering in a more positive light.

Life on the Balearic Islands has been able to adapt to the economic and political demands of the new, emerging Europe, but at the same time has managed to stay true to the human and social values that are the essence of Mediterranean culture. The quality of life is, without doubt, in large part due to the weather and the natural spectacle of the land. However, it goes further: the relationships between the people are easy-going, optimistic and creative, three characteristics which produce solutions for any situation that may arise and avoid getting stuck in a rut.

The presence of so many central Europeans on the islands is proof of this: not only do they enjoy a warm climate, in addition they benefit from a more intelligently paced life style. The siesta is possible and the

ken zu lassen. Eine idyllische Landschaft lässt uns Sorgen und Nöte vergessen und hilft uns, die Dinge in einem positiven Licht zu sehen.

Die Menschen auf den Balearen haben es verstanden, die menschlichen und gesellschaftlichen Werte, die den Kern der mediterranen Kultur darstellen, zu retten und zu bewahren, obwohl sie ihre Lebensweise an die wirtschaftlichen und politischen Erfordernisse des neuen Europas angepasst haben. Es handelt sich um eine Lebensqualität, die unzweifelhaft vom Klima und den Naturschönheiten beeinflusst ist. Doch darüber hinaus hat sich ein ungezwungenes lebendiges und kreatives System zwischenmenschlicher Beziehungen erhalten, das Auswege aus dem täglichen Trott und Lösungen in festgefahrenen Situationen bietet.

Ein Beweis dafür ist der Zustrom von Mitteleuropäern auf die Inseln, wo sie, außer dass sie das

unruffled reply “we will see” is permitted when confronted with certain problems. These are manifestations of the islanders' calmness and level-headedness. Human contact should not be undervalued: the islanders are straightforward and open people, something which makes the visitor enjoy their stay and the sense of well-being the islands give off even more.

The Balearic archipelago, in the Mediterranean, is made up of three main islands: Mallorca, Menorca and Ibiza. We use the Catalan, or Spanish, places names and so Mallorca, Majorca in Spanish, appears. Two other islands, Cabrera and Formentera, are much smaller. There are over one hundred islets. In ancient times Mallorca, Menorca and Cabrera were known as the Gimnesias Islands, and Ibiza and Formentera were referred to as the Pitiusas Islands.

The history books reveal that the first settlers on the Balearic Islands came on ships from other

warme Klima genießen können, einen entspannteren Lebensstil vorfinden, in dem die Siesta und das “ja veurem” (“wir werden sehen”) als sorglose Reaktionen auf kniffelige Situationen untrennbar mit der Landschaft dieser Insel der Ruhe verbunden sind. Auch darf man den Kontakt mit den Menschen nicht außer Acht lassen; die Inselbewohner sind offene Menschen, die großen Einfluss darauf haben, dass man den Augenblick genießt und schon nach kurzer Zeit von einem Gefühl der Zufriedenheit durchströmt wird.

Das Territorium des Archipels der Balearen in der Mitte des westlichen Mittelmeeres setzt sich aus fünf größeren Inseln – Mallorca, Menorca, Cabrera, Ibiza und Formentera – sowie einigen Hundert kleineren Inseln und Eilanden zusammen. Von alters her sind die drei erstgenannten als Islas Gimnésias und die beiden anderen als Islas Pitiusas bekannt.

Mediterranean islands and from the countries of the east. Consequently the culture has always been intrinsically linked to the sea and shipping. Sailing expeditions seeking metals and other commodities, or trading contacts, have played an important role in the evolution of the way of life. The islands' strategic location on the sea routes between Italy and the Iberian peninsula, halfway between Africa and Europe, favored the development of a stable colony of seafarers. Mythical tales talk about the search for precious metals by the Greeks. After the Phoenicians, the Carthaginians and the Greeks, all of whom dominated the islands, came the Romans, one hundred and twenty three years before Christ.

The conquest of the Balearics by the Arabs in 902 A.D. and the islands' incorporation into the sphere of influence of the emirate of Cordoba brought changes to society and culture. This ascendancy remained unaltered until the thirteenth century when the islands

Die Geschichte berichtet von den ersten Eroberern der Balearen, die mit Schiffen von anderen Mittelmeerinseln und den Völkern des Orients kamen. Hierin liegen die Ursprünge für eine Kultur, deren Lebensweise im Grunde immer vom Meer abhing: Streifzüge von Seefahrern auf der Suche nach Metallen und anderen Rohstoffen sowie Handelsbeziehungen waren von entscheidender Bedeutung. Die strategische Lage der Balearen auf den Seerouten zwischen der italienischen und der iberischen Halbinsel sowie zwischen zwei Kontinenten – Afrika und Europa – förderte die Ansiedlung von Seefahrern; diese reicht weit in der Zeit zurück. Die Sagen erzählen von der Suche der Griechen nach Edelmetallen; Phönizier, Karthager und Griechen wechselten sich in der Herrschaft über die Inseln ab, bis sie 123 v.Chr. unter die Kontrolle der Römer fielen.

Die Eroberung der Balearen durch die Muselmanen im Jahre 902 und die Eingliederung ins

were again invaded, this time by Jaume I from Catalonia. This was a turning point in the islands' history as they were integrated into the Christian, western world and adopted the Catalan language.

At the same time, on the European mainland a new, architectural style, gothic, that would deeply mark all that came after, was making itself felt. The trends and techniques in fashion on the continent determined the islands' physiognomy, though of course modified by their own regional peculiarities.

Over the centuries the islands have changed radically, but in the sixties and seventies of the twentieth century a new modernizing force arrived on the scene: the boom in tourism. The traditional, rural society was compelled to become a modern, urban one with the consequent changes in infrastructures and building developments. The main cities, especially the capital Palma de Mallorca, and the tourist

Emirat von Cordoba brachten viele Veränderungen in der Kultur und der Gesellschaft mit sich. Die arabische Vormachtstellung blieb nahezu ungebrochen bis zur Eroberung durch die Katalanen unter König Jaume I. im 13. Jahrhundert. Dieser Herrschaftswechsel markiert einen Wendepunkt in der neueren Geschichte der Inseln, denn sie werden damit in die christliche, westliche Welt integriert und übernehmen die katalanische Sprache.

Zur selben Zeit entwickelte sich in Europa mit der Gotik ein neuer Baustil, der die spätere Architektur maßgeblich prägte. Die folgenden Stile und Moden, die die westliche Welt erlebte, spiegeln sich im Antlitz der Inseln mit ihren je eigenen regionalen Besonderheiten wider.

Zu den tiefgehenden Veränderungen, die die Balearen im Laufe der Jahrtausende erlebt haben, muss man auch die der sechziger und siebziger

projects along the coasts have come to the forefront while other zones have been pushed into the background, often fortunately as they have thus remained preserved in another time and world.

These differences between zones are why this book deals with life on the islands in three separate chapters, there being a special emphasis on Mallorca: life in the city of Palma, life in the countryside and life on the coast. In each chapter the different landscapes are shown, what life is like there, and finally a selection of the best and most delightful homes, flats and hotels is offered.

Jahre des vergangenen Jahrhunderts zählen. Der in diesen Jahrzehnten einsetzende Tourismus-Boom sorgte für einen fundamentalen Wandel. Diese erneute Wende ist nichts anderes, als der Schritt von einer klassischen Agrargesellschaft zu einer modernen Gesellschaft, die zwangsläufig auch die Besiedlung und Infrastruktur verändert hat. So rückten die großen Städte wie Palma de Mallorca und weitere Tourismuszentren entlang der Küsten in den Vordergrund. Andere Gebiete wurden dagegen vernachlässigt, wenig modernisiert und konnten somit ihre Ursprünglichkeit bewahren.

Das vorliegende Buch möchte die verschiedenen Facetten der Balearen vor Augen führen und lädt dazu ein, das Leben auf diesen Inseln neu kennen zu lernnen. Das Leben in der Stadt, das Leben auf dem Land und das Leben am Meer sind die Stationen dieser Reise über Mallorca und die übrigen Balearen. Anhand außergewöhnlicher Fotografien wird der Reiz der jeweiligen Landschaften und ihrer typischen Lebensweisen ebenso gezeigt wie eine Auswahl traumhafter Häuser, Wohnungen und einladender Hotels.

LIVING IN THE CITY

LEBEN IN DER STADT

Living in the City

This magnificent, beautiful walled city sits on a bay of warm, transparent waters that throw back the reflections of hundreds of masts of the yachts gently rocking in the harbor and of the shimmering immutable buildings themselves. The bay of Palma is today characterized by the gardened promenade along the seafront and the imposing elegance of the emblematic architecture which receives the intense, reflected sunlight off the water. Thus Palma is symbolized by the outline of La Seu cathedral, watched over from afar by the legendary Bellver castle.

The current name of the city goes back to the eighteenth century. In maps and documents of ancient times it was known as Ciutat de Mallorques. When the Arabs arrived they called it Madina Mayurga. The archeological remains found in the ground allow the city's history to be traced back to the establishment of the first Roman camps on the seashore. The city in the times of the Arabs and Berbers was never greater than under the Roman empire. However, two centuries later, the need to obtain a stable water supply pushed the city planners into extending the city walls so they could be used as an aqueduct. Without realizing it they were outlining the city as it was to be at the beginning of the twentieth century. The most representative remains of the period of Arab occupation are the baths in the old part of the city. The gothic cathedral, la Seu, was constructed on the site of the principal mosque, and the Almudaina palace went up where el alcazar (a Moorish fortress) used to be.

Until the fifteenth century the city limits were left untouched. The city wall went round what today is the beltway around Palma, the avingudes and passeig Mallorca. Later the Roman wall was replaced by the renaissance wall, sadly demolished by municipal decree in 1901 to make way for the Calvet plan. Fortunately the Baluard de Sant Pere (Bastion of Saint Peter) and the stretch from el Mirador to Baluard del Príncep have been conserved.

Another important architectural intervention was the shifting of the Torrent de la Riera, which divided the city in two, in the seventeenth century. This made it possible to reorganize the city based on two main thoroughfares, el paseo del Born and la Rambla, both still existing today.

Leben in der Stadt

Palma, diese wunderbare, schöne, von einer alten Mauer umgebene Stadt, liegt in einer weiten Bucht, deren warme, transparente Gewässer sie sanft umspülen. In diesem Meer spiegeln sich Tausende von Masten der verschiedensten Segelboote und versetzen die Silhouette dieser unerschütterlichen Stadt in Bewegung. Heute wird die Bucht von Palma im Wesentlichen vom langen, begrünten Paseo Marítimo geprägt, der von den Fassaden vieler charakteristischer Gebäude gesäumt ist, die sich den Strahlen einer unnachgiebigen Sonne aussetzen. Sie selbst jedoch, Palma, identifiziert sich am stärksten mit der gezackten Linie ihrer prächtigen Kathedrale, la Seu, und wird von Weitem von der legendären Festung Bellver überwacht.

Der heutige Name der mallorquinischen Hauptstadt stammt aus dem 18. Jahrhundert. Auf alten Karten und in historischen Dokumenten wurde sie als Ciutat de Mallorques bezeichnet; später, während der muselmanischen Herrschaft, bekam sie den Namen Madina Mayurqa. Anhand der erhaltenen Überreste kann man die Spuren ihrer Geschichte von der Errichtung der ersten römischen Sied-lungen am Ufer des Meeres verfolgen. Die Araber und Berber hielten sich an die Grenzen der römischen Stadtmauern, aber die Notwendigkeit der Wasserversorgung führte dazu, dass fast zwei Jahrhunderte später der von Mauern umschlossene Bereich erweitert wurde und die Mauern als Aquädukt genutzt wurden. So errichtete man damals, ohne es zu wissen, eine Mauer, welche die Stadt zu Beginn des 20. Jahrhunderts begrenzen sollte. Von der muselmanischen Besetzung sind als repräsentativstes Überbleibsel die arabischen Bäder erhalten; sie liegen in der Altstadt. Über der wichtigsten Moschee im Stadtkern wurde die gotische Kathedrale, la Seu, errichtet, und auf den Resten der arabischen Festung der Almudaina-Palast.

Bis ins 15. Jahrhundert blieb der Grundriss der Stadt unverändert. Die Stadtmauer verlief dort, wo heute die Umgehungsstraßen Palma umrunden: die Avingudes und der Paseo Mallorca. Später wurde die römische Mauer durch eine im Renaissance-Stil ersetzt, die leider aufgrund einer im Rahmen des Plan Calvet

Main façade of the Palau de l'Almudaina.

Hauptfassade des Almudaina-Palastes.

However, charming as all this may be, the building that best symbolizes Palma is la Seu gothic cathedral, constructed in various stages between the fourteenth and sixteenth centuries. It is reasonable to believe that the initial project was modified around 1350 and instead of just one nave three were then planned. The already constructed apse was conserved and the height and width of the first project were increased. Fifty years on, work was started on el Portal del Mirador on the sea-facing front, an unsurpassable example of how gothic architecture evolved on the island. The final result, clearly visible from outside, is artistically and aesthetically interesting: the rhythmic succession of buttresses, flying buttresses and the bell towers give rise to a singular overall effect in which each individual element, and its contribution to the whole, has been carefully weighed up.

In the nineteenth and twentieth centuries there were two further modifications to the cathedral. In 1851 an earthquake brought down the western façade, although everything could later be restored, except for the Portal Major. The second reform was carried out by the famous architect Antoni Gaudí at the dawn of the twentieth century when he modified the areas of public worship, moving the choir from the center of the nave to the presbytery. Today the Mallorcan painter Miquel Barceló is working on another remodeling.

In front of la Seu there stands the Almudaina palace, an old fortress that was fitted out to be the residence of the kings and queens of Mallorca. It was extended using as a model Perpignan castle in France, although its square towers are a throwback to Moorish design. When the Catalan reign came to an end, the building fell into disrepair until eventually, at the close of the nineteenth century, its restoration was undertaken. The primitive torre del Ángel, the Santa Aina chapel with its romanic portal and the Saló del Tinell are especially worthy of note.

The city of Palma is made up of a series of plaças and different quarters which join together to give it its special character. The plaça major (main square) is a shopping area, principally for clothes, which runs up to the traditional Olivar food market. On the other side it extends up to la avenida de Jaume III, where more upmarket garments and brands are found. The final boundary of this zone is marked off by la plaça de Cort containing the city hall and the parliament. Leading out of this square is Argentería street, full of little jewelry shops which make imitations and pieces in silver among other things. The central part of the city with so many cafés, bars, restaurants, antique shops and art galleries dotted around is the busiest area of the old city.

(1901) durchgeführten Stadterneuerung niedergerissen wurde. Von ihr stehen heute noch der Baluard de Sant Pere und das Stück zwischen dem Mirador und dem Baluard del Princep.

Ein wichtiger Eingriff war die Umleitung des Torrent de la Riera im 17. Jahrhundert. Dieses nur nach starken Regenfällen gefüllte Flussbett teilte die Stadt in zwei Teile. Daraufhin konnte die Unterstadt anhand zweier Hauptachsen ausgerichtet werden: dem Paseo del Born und der Rambla. Beide sind nach wie vor wichtige Verkehrswege.

Aber das Symbol der Stadt, das Bauwerk, mit dem Palma am ehesten in Verbindung gebracht wird, ist la Seu. Diese gotische Kathedrale wurde in mehreren Etappen vom 14. bis ins 16. Jahrhundert gebaut. Nach einer der herrschenden Meinungen wurde der ursprüngliche Entwurf in der Mitte des 14. Jahrhunderts abgeändert und die Kathedrale von einem auf drei Schiffe erweitert. Die bereits errichtete Apsis blieb erhalten und die Höhe und Breite des ersten Entwurfs wurden korrigiert. Am Ende des selben Jahrhunderts wurden die Arbeiten für das Portal del Mirador angefangen, das an der dem Meer zugewandten Fassade liegt. Es ist ein beispielloses Zeugnis von der Entwicklung der Gotik auf der Insel. Die Kathedrale ist von hohem künstlerischem und ästhetischem Wert, besonders im Hinblick auf die äußere architektonische Struktur, in der die rhythmische Folge der Strebe- und Zierpfeiler, die sich von den Glockentürmen aus entwickeln, ein einzigartiges und unnachahmliches Ensemble bildet.

Einige der späteren Eingriffe an der Kathedrale sollte man hervorheben. Die erste datiert aus dem Jahr 1851, als ein Erdbeben die gesamte Westfassade bis auf das Portal Major zum Einsturz brachte – sie wurde später rekonstruiert. Der zweite erfolgte zu Beginn des 20. Jahrhunderts durch die Hand von Antoni Gaudí. Er erneuerte den Innenaufbau, indem er den Chor aus der Mitte des Hauptschiffes in das Presbyterium verlegte. Die neueste Gestaltung ist die, an der der mallorquinische Maler Miquel Barceló zurzeit arbeitet.

Gegenüber von la Seu liegt der Almudaina-Palast, eine alte Festung, die zur Residenz der Könige von Mallorca umgebaut wurde. Sie wurde nach dem Modell des Schlosses von Perpignan (Frankreich) erweitert, auch wenn ihre Türme mit quadratischem Grundriss ein Erbe der Muselmanen sind. Nach dem Ende des katalanischen Königreiches verfiel das Gebäude nach und nach, bis man Ende des 19. Jahrhunderts mit der Restaurierung begann. Besonders interessant sind der Turm Torre del Ángel, die Kapelle Santa Aina mit ihrem romanischen Portal und der Empfangssaal Saló del Tinell.

Die Stadt setzt sich aus vielen Stadtvierteln, die sich um kleine Plätze gruppieren und jeweils einen ganz eigenen Charakter haben, zusammen. Die Plaza Major ist eine Einkaufszone mit vielen Modegeschäften, die sich zu einer Seite bis zum alten Wochenmarkt Mercado del Olivar erstreckt. Zur anderen Seite führt sie zur Avenida de Jaume III, wo sich die teureren Boutiquen befinden, und mündet schließlich, wenn man der Straße Calle Argentaria folgt, in der sich viele kleine Schmuckgeschäfte aneinander reihen, die vor allem Silber- und Modeschmuck herstellen, in die Plaza de Cort. Hier befinden sich das Rathaus und das Parlamentsgebäude. Überall in diesen belebten Straßen und Seitengassen der Altstadt stößt man auf Cafés, Kneipen, Restaurants, Antiquitätenhändler, Kunstgalerien und vieles mehr, das zum Verweilen und Stöbern einlädt.

When evening falls the medieval Bellver castle is silhouetted against the sky, watching over the city of Palma.

In der Dämmerung wacht die Silhouette der mittelalterlichen Festung Bellver über die Bucht von Palma.

The entrance to the Gran Hotel, a modernist construction by the architect Domènech i Montaner. Besides housing the permanent collection of the painter Anglada Camarasa it is also used for temporary expositions.

Eingang des Gran Hotel, einem Jugendstilbau des Architekten Doménech i Montaner. Neben der ständigen Sammlung des Malers Anglada Camarasa werden hier wechselnde Kunstausstellungen gezeigt.

Del 17 de juliol al
26 d'agost
Fundació "la Caixa"

City Landscapes
Stadtlandschaften

City Landscapes

The more than manageable dimensions of the city mean that it is possible to visit most of the sites in the old part on foot. If you set out from el paseo del Born or la Rambla, you will be strolling along tree-lined streets packed with small-shops, bars dating back decades, tiny restaurants and numerous art galleries. Heading off into the alley-like streets with time to spare is the best way of seeing the city, savoring it and observing how local people go about their daily business.

The charm and elegance of the patios of the houses of the nobility are one of the most endearing features of the old quarter of Palma and attract many visitors. The style of each building can vary depending on the trends prevailing when it was conceived, but all of them are the work of designers who knew how to combine artistic inspiration with practical necessity in a city that kept abreast of the times.

Many houses of the nobility were extended by incorporating the house next door into the plan. Fine examples of how this can be done are the baroque patios dating from the seventeenth and eighteenth century of houses such as Can Vivot and Can Oleza, which were constructed over ancient medieval structures. In contrast, Solleric palace is an example of a nobleman's house specifically designed according to local practices under the sway of Italian and French baroque. It has now been converted into an exposition center for contemporary art, owned by Palma city hall. Many other art galleries and private foundations are housed in similarly impressive buildings.

The Gran Hotel was one of the first on the island which revealed the business sector's unwavering belief in the future of tourism as a way forward. It is a modernist design by the architect Domènech i Montaner dating from 1901, since converted into the cultural center of a banking enterprise. Its modernism does not stand alone for it is near other representative modernist buildings from the same period.

Stadtlandschaften

Das Zentrum der Stadt ist so bemessen, dass man zu den meisten Punkten bequem zu Fuß gelangt. Wenn man am Paseo del Born oder der Rambla losgeht, findet man in ihrem von Bäumen gesäumten Verlauf ungezählte Geschäfte, beliebte traditionelle Cafés, kleine Restaurants und viele, viele Kunstgalerien. Einfach aufs Geratewohl losbummeln, sich in den Gassen verlieren, ist der beste Tipp, um diese Stadt kennen zu lernen, sie zu genießen und sich von ihren Lebensrhythmus anstecken zu lassen.

Der Zauber und die Eleganz der Innenhöfe der alten Herrschaftshäuser charakterisieren das Herz des alten Palma und gehören zu den meistbesuchten Sehenswürdigkeiten. Man kann die Stilrichtungen, von denen sie sich haben inspirieren lassen, an ihrer Gestaltung gut ablesen. Die wahren Meister unter den lokalen Architekten und Handwerkern schafften es jedoch, gekonnt bestimmte Stilschemata an die Gebräuche und Erfordernisse einer Stadt anzupassen, die sich ständig weiterentwickelt.

Viele der Herrschaftshäuser wurden durch Zusammenschluss mit den angrenzenden Gebäuden erweitert. In diesem Zusammenhang muss man besonders auf die Innenhöfe des Barock hinweisen, die im 17. und 18. Jahrhundert auf alten mittelalterlichen Strukturen errichtet wurden, wie im Can Vivot oder Can Oleza. Im Gegensatz dazu stellt der Palacio Solleric ein Beispiel für ein neu errichtetes Adelshaus dar, das den Normen der lokalen Bautradition folgt und Einflüsse des französischen und italienischen Barock aufweist. Heute wird er als Ausstellungszentrum für zeitgenössische Kunst der Stadt Palma genutzt. Überhaupt sind viele private Stiftungen und Kunstgalerien in diesen majestätischen Gebäuden eingerichtet.

Das Gran Hotel gehört zu den ersten Hotels der Insel, die blind auf den Tourismus als Zukunftsperspektive vertrauten. Es ist ein Bau des Jugendstils, katalanisch "modernisme", aus dem Jahr 1901 des Architekten Doménech i Montaner und wird heute als Kulturstiftung von einer Bank genutzt. In seiner Nähe stehen weitere Jugendstilhäuser, die ein Bild dieser Epoche vermitteln.

The structure and beauty of la Seu as it rises out of the mist is a symbol of the city of Palma.

In all ihrer Größe und Schönheit taucht hier die Kathedrale la Seu, Symbol der Stadt Palma, aus dem Morgendunst auf.

La Seu and the Palau de l'Almudaina represent an important part of the history and culture of the Balearic Islands. This side view of the gothic cathedral allows some of its most characteristic features to be admired.

La Seu und der Almudaina-Palast spielen eine wesentliche Rolle in der Geschichte und Kultur der Balearen. Die charakteristischen Merkmale der gotischen Kathedrale eröffnen sich dem Betrachter am besten von Südosten.

The defining rhythm and expressive power of the cathedral come from the accelerating succession of these magnificent flying buttresses and buttresses topped off with pinnacles.

Rhythmus und Ausdruckskraft dieses sakralen Bauwerks rühren von der dichten Abfolge der Strebe- und Zierpfeiler her, die mit Zinnen abschließen.

Meandering through the old part of the city enables the visitor to get to know the remains of the old wall and the city's rich cultural and architectural heritage.

Auf einem Spaziergang durch die Altstadt kann der Besucher die noch erhaltenen Abschnitte der Stadtmauer und den Reichtum an Kultur und Denkmälern dieses Stadtviertels kennen lernen.

Some of the changes made to the urban landscape over the last few years have given back to the city important open spaces such as the Park de la Mar, Ses Volts, L'hort del Rei and the Paseo along the Murada, among others. The townsfolk of Palma can now recreate themselves in the open air, taking a breather as they saunter through the city.

In den vergangenen Jahren konnten durch einige der städtebaulichen Projekte, wichtige Grünanlagen für die Stadt Palma zurückgewonnen werden, wie unter anderen der Parc de la Mar, Ses Voltes, l'Hort del Rei und der Passeig damunt la Murada (Spazierweg auf der Stadtmauer). Die weitläufigen Plätze und Anlagen laden gleichermaßen die Einheimischen Palmesanos wie ihre Gäste zum Bummeln und Genießen ein.

The emblematic Castell de Bellver, dating from the gothic period, is unique among Medieval Spanish architecture due to its very conception and its geometry. Out of a perfectly round circle rise up three towers while a fourth one, visible in the photo, is joined by an arch. During the eighteenth and nineteenth centuries it served as a prison where the writer Gaspar Melchor de Jovellanos ended and wrote a monograph on the castle. Today you can visit the Museu de la Ciutat inside the castle.

Die beeindruckende Königsburg Castell de Bellver ist aufgrund ihrer Konzeption und Geometrie ein einzigartiges Bauwerk der spanischen mittelalterlichen Gotik. Ein perfekter Kreis mit drei angegliederten Türmen definiert den Grundriss; ein vierter, hier zu sehen, ist durch einen Bogen mit dem Ensemble verbunden. Im 18. und 19. Jahrhundert wurde Bellver als Gefängnis benutzt, der Schriftsteller Gaspar Melchor de Jovellanos hielt sich hier auf und verfasste eine Monographie der Anlage. Heute kann man in seinen Mauern das Stadtmuseum, Museu de la Ciutat, besuchen.

Sa Llotja, the old headquarters of the guild of Merchants, was the last great gothic building erected in Mallorca. It was the work of the masterful Guillem Sagrera.

Sa Llotja, eine alte Niederlassung der Handelsbörse, ist das jüngste gotische Werk in Mallorca; es wurde von Meister Guillem Sagrera errichtet.

1919

Frasquet
J. Casasayas
BOMBONS

Can Cassavas and the Pensión Menorquina are modernist designs by Francesc Roca. Located in the center of Palma, they are two symmetrical buildings separated by a narrow street (left).

The Gran Hotel stands very near by, an architectural oeuvre which heralded the beginning of a modernist epoch on the island. The prime mover behind it, Domènech i Montaner, would later go on to create grand and preeminent buildings in Barcelona, such as the Palau de la Música and the Casa Lleó Morera (right).

Previous pages: In the center of Palma there are some modernist buildings. In these photos their resplendent compositional designs are clearly visible.

Can Casasayas und die Pensión Menorquina sind Entwürfe des Architekten Francesc Roca. Das Ensemble in der Altstadt Palmas besteht aus zwei symmetrischen Gebäuden, die durch eine schmale Gasse getrennt sind (links).

Ganz in der Nähe befindet sich das Gran Hotel, ein Bauwerk, das die Jugendstil-Epoche auf der Insel einleitete. Sein Schöpfer entwarf später in Barcelona einige Gebäude, die zu großem Ruhm gelangten, wie der Palau de la Música oder das Haus Casa Lleó Morera (rechts).

Auf den vorigen Seiten: Im Zentrum Palmas trifft man auf beeindruckend schöne Jugendstil-Gebäude, auf katalanisch Modernisme genannt.

Other trends coming immediately before the modernist movement are reflected in the façades of some high-level buildings. One example is the neomudéjar, which can be seen at Can Corbella (right).

Andere Stilrichtungen, die dem Jugendstil unmittelbar vorausgingen, spiegeln sich in der Fassadengestaltung einiger bekannter Gebäude wider, wie hier im Can Corbella der Neomudéjar-Stil, der von der arabischen Ornamentik inspiriert ist (rechts).

Museu d'Art Espanyol Contemporani
Palma de Mallorca
Fundación Juan March
COL·LECCIÓ PERMANENT
EXPOSICIÓ TEMPORAL

Previous pages: These pictures showing the patios of noblemen's houses in the old part of the city give an idea of how overlapping artistic styles from distinct periods have left their mark on this fantastic city.

The architect Guillem Reynés designed the house of the banker Joan March in 1916. Today it is the headquarters of the Museum of Contemporary Spanish Art.

Auf den vorigen Seiten: Einige der patios (Innenhöfe) der Herrschaftshäuser, die man in der Altstadt findet, zeigen deutlich die Überlagerung verschiedener Epochen und ihrer künstlerischen Stile; sie alle sind Teil dieser wunderbaren Stadt.

Der Architekt Guillem Reynés entwarf im Jahre 1916 das Haus des Bankiers Joan March, das heute Sitz des Museums für zeitgenössische spanische Kunst ist.

The façade of one of the buildings giving out onto the city's sea front can be seen in the upper photo. The magnificent loggia, with its seven arches, stone columns and Ionic capitals, dates back to the eighteenth century.

Eines der weltlichen Gebäude, die die Silhouette der Stadt zum Meer hin prägen, ist die auf dem oberen Foto sichtbare Loggia mit sieben Bögen aus steinernen Säulen mit ionischen Kapitellen; sie stammt aus dem 18. Jahrhundert.

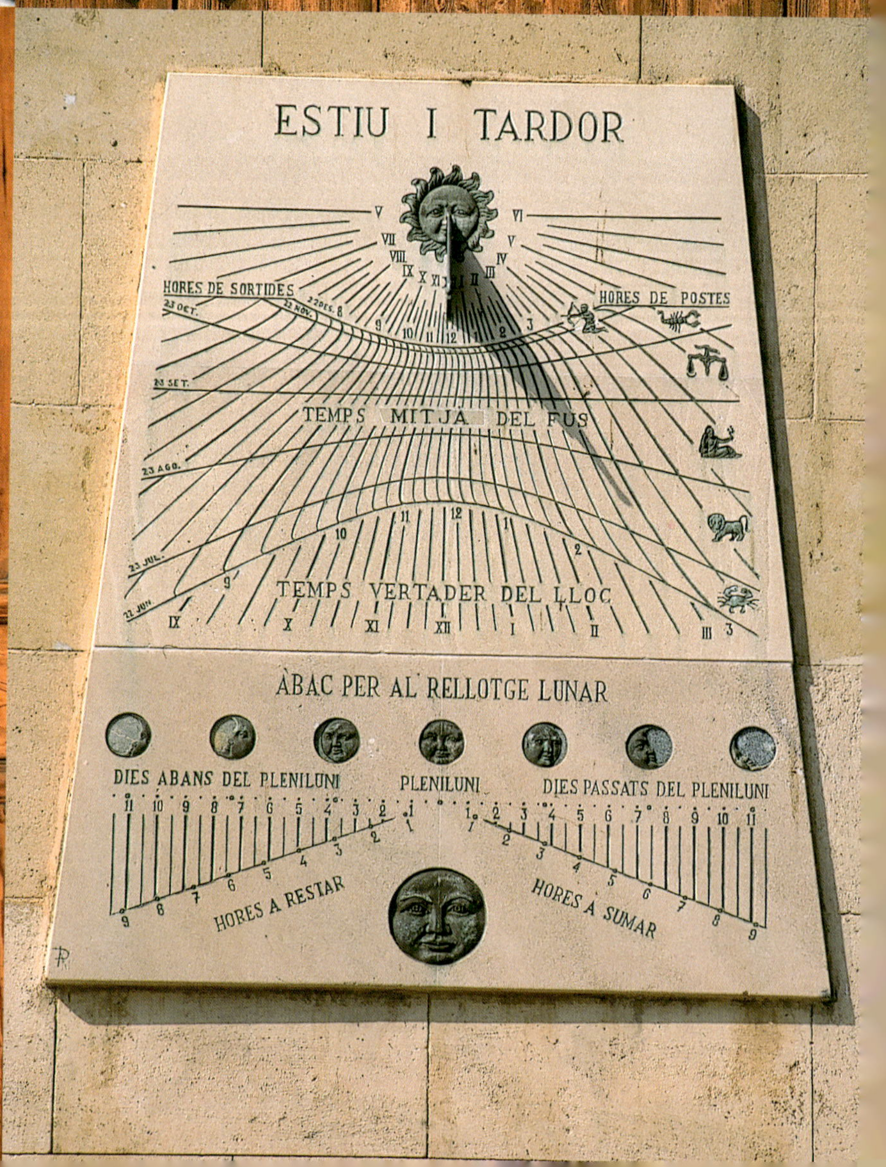
ESTIU I TARDOR
HORES DE SORTIDES
HORES DE POSTES
TEMPS MITJÀ DEL FUS
TEMPS VERTADER DEL LLOC
ÀBAC PER AL RELLOTGE LUNAR
DIES ABANS DEL PLENILUNI
PLENILUNI
DIES PASSATS DEL PLENILUNI
HORES A RESTAR
HORES A SUMAR

27

The historic center of the city is irresistibly attractive for any tourist who likes to wander. They will find that the area abounds in impressive architect, both on religious buildings and civil ones. The Palacio de la Diputación, the work of Joaquim Pavia and today the headquarters of the Consell Insular de Mallorca, shows how the neogothic trend pushed its way to the forefront at the end of the nineteenth century.

Das historische Stadtzentrum bietet sich zum ausgedehnten Bummeln an, wobei der Besucher die wichtigsten Werke religiöser und weltlicher Architektur der Insel entdecken kann. Der Palacio de la Diputación von Joaquim Pavia ist heute Sitz des Inselrates von Mallorca und ein Beispiel für den Triumph des neogotischen Stils am Ende des 19. Jahrhunderts.

Outdoor Living: in the City

Draussen Leben: in der Stadt

Outdoor Living: In the City

Antoni Maura avenue, el paseo del Born and la Rambla are the roads leading into the old city from the parque del Mar, gardens where there is an enormous lake, providing a buffer zone around the cathedral. Behind, between the city walls, there is a space known as Ses voltes where open air theatre is staged. Beneath the vaults of the walls, expositions are held.

As you go up el Born you will come to an entrance to a garden, el Hort del Rei (the king's kitchen garden), where the townsfolk can enjoy the open air in a well-groomed garden setting with fountains. This green space in the center of the city is embellished by the presence of sculptures by recognized artists such as Miró, Subirachs, Calder and Roselló.

Another building steeped in history is Sa Llotja, the old gothic style merchants' headquarters, today used as another exposition center by the city hall. Located on the waterfront, this building is the work of the same designer responsible for el Portal del Mirador of la Seu cathedral, Guillem Sagrera. It is one of the gothic masterpieces of Mallorca.

Not far away there are enchanting eateries, cafés and bars for a meal, snack, tapas, or just a drink while scanning the bay. This area is also a hub for night-time socializing. The young natives and tourists take the bay as their starting point and make their way to the city center dropping in at the different bars. Such is the coming and going that the neighbors sometimes find it difficult to get to sleep. Top rate live music is also performed in some of the small clubs around the area.

No tourist need limit him or herself to just the city and its monuments; the culture, folklore and traditions of the people can also be explored by visiting the fiestas of the outlying towns and villages, and experiencing first hand these collective celebrations. One of the most colorful and vibrant festivals in Palma is la fiesta de Sant Sebastià, the city's patron, held in mid-January. Its origins go back to the fifteenth century, a time when Christian devotion surged on the island, fostered by the teachings of Ramón Llull in favor of the unity of the faith. The prayers and the processions in the Saint's honor were specifically aimed at seeking protection from epidemics and plagues. Although especially associated with Palma, the celebrations also take place in towns like Costitx, Muro, Sa Pobla, Alcúdia and Inca.

On the eve of the fiesta, bonfires are lit in the plaças around the city, and then the locals enjoy a real feast of good food and wine until they are satiated. The night then becomes even more lively with music and dancing almost until the sun comes up. It is the most important winter fiesta and is closely linked to the pagan celebration of the winter solstice. The following day a richly varied procession of animals parades in front of an image of the saint and all of them are blessed. Dressed up with bright ribbons, they then follow a pre-established route to the delight of the cheering little children.

The parque de la Mar, Ses Voltes and the avinguda de Antoni Maura are often ideal scenarios for large-scale outdoor events. Fireworks, concerts, plays, dances and even films are shown during the summer season, bringing together people from the city and those from outside, the Part Forana.

Draussen leben: in der Stadt

Die Avinguda Antoni Maura, der Passeig del Born und die Rambla führen vom Parc de la Mar aus in die Altstadt. Dieser Park mit seinem großflächigen Teich bildet eine Pufferzone um die Kathedrale herum. Dahinter befindet sich zwischen den Stadtmauern Ses Voltes; dies ist eine Anlage mit einem Freilufttheater und einem Ausstellungsraum in dem überdachtem Gang, der auf der Stadtmauer angelegt wurde.

Wenn man über den Passeig del Born Richtung Stadt geht, stößt man auf den begrünten Eingang zum Park Hort del Rei (Gemüsegarten des Königs). Diese herrlich gepflegte Grünanlage ist ein idealer Quell der Ruhe und Erfrischung für die Palmesanos mit ihrem Schmuck aus Brunnen, Fontänen und Ziergärten. In dieser grünen Lunge der Stadt wurden viele Skulpturen international anerkannter Künstler aufgestellt, so z.B. von Miró, Subirachs, Calder und Roselló.

Zu den Sehenswürdigkeiten gehört auf jeden Fall auch Sa Llotja, eine alte Handelsbörse im gotischen Stil, die heute als Ausstellungssaal der Stadt Palma genutzt wird. Dieses Gebäude am Passeig Marítim ist ein Werk des Baumeisters Guillem Sagrera, der auch am Portal del Mirador der Kathedrale mitgewirkt hat. Sa Llotja ist unbestreitbar eines der Meisterwerke der mallorquinischen Gotik.

In der Umgebung warten die verschiedensten Lokale darauf, entdeckt zu werden; neben Speisen und Getränken bieten sie eine herrliche Aussicht auf die Bucht von Palma. Dies ist auch das Stadtviertel zum Ausgehen: Der Passeig Marítim bildet den Ausgangspunkt, und von hier in Richtung Zentrum kehren die jungen Leute in einer Bar nach der nächsten ein, so dass das ständige Kommen und Gehen so manchen Nachbarn um den Schlaf bringt. In einigen der kleinen Kneipen und Clubs in dieser Ecke kann man auch hervorragende Live-Konzerte hören.

Außer der Stadt selbst mit ihren Denkmälern kann man die Kultur, die Folklore und die Sitten und Gebräuche eines Volkes auch gut im Rahmen der regionalen Feste kennen lernen, wenn sich das gesellschaftliche Zusammenleben vor den Augen aller abspielt. Eines der schönsten Feste ist das des Sant Sebastià, des Stadtpatrons, das Mitte Januar abgehalten wird. Seine Ursprünge gehen bis auf das 15. Jahrhundert zurück, als sich auf der Insel der christliche Glaube ausbreitete, für den sich mit vielen Worten der Philosoph und Schriftgelehrte Ramon Llull eingesetzt hatte. Die Gebete und Prozessionen zu Ehren des Heiligen hatten ein ganz konkretes Ziel: den Schutz des Patrons vor Seuchen und Krankheiten zu erbitten. Dieses Fest wird in Palma mit besonderer Begeisterung gefeiert, aber auch in anderen Ortschaften der Insel wie Costitx, Muro, Sa Pobla, Alcúdia, Inca ...

Der Parc de la Mar, Ses Voltes und die Avenida de Antoni Maura bilden auch häufig die Bühne für die großen populären Volksfeste. Feuerwerke, Musikkonzerte, Theatervorstellungen, Folklore und Freiluftkino sind einige der Veranstaltungen, zu denen sich in den Sommermonaten die Menschen der Stadt mit denen der anderen Inselteile, der Part Forana, vereinen.

PALMA

Near Palma lie some beautiful gardens – the grounds of an old possessió dwelling – waiting to be visited. Around Bunyola, one can find highly aesthetic gardens such as Alfàbia, Raixa and Sa Granja in Esporles.

Nicht weit von Palma liegen die zauberhaften Gärten einiger alter Landgüter als schönes Ausflugsziel. Dazu zählen die besonders hübschen Anlagen von Alfabia und Raixa in Bunyola oder Sa Granja in Esporles.

The Passeig Marítim which runs from the city to the port's wharfs to the west was extended to the Portixol zone lying to the east. The result is that sports and fresh air lovers can work out – biking, skating, jogging or simply lazily strolling by the sea-against an amazing backdrop.

Der Passeig Marítim verbindet die Stadt mit den Hafenmolen im Westen und wurde inzwischen bis Portixol im Osten verlängert, so dass den Sportlichen heute ein unvergleichlich schönes Trainingsgelände zur Verfügung steht, um Fahrrad zu fahren, Rollschuh zu laufen, zu joggen oder einfach nur ausgiebige Spaziergänge zu machen.

Nearly all the way round the bay of Palma there are many boating clubs and clubhouses, the Real Club Náutico de Palma, the Club de Mar and the Port Marina de Mallorca being specially worthy of mention. Other, smaller ones even more geared to sailing such as El Portixol, El Molinar and Cala Gamba are a few minutes away.

Mehrere Yachthäfen säumen die Bucht von Palma, dazu gehören der Real Club Náutico de Palma, der Club de Mar und el Port Marina de Mallorca. Etwas weiter vom Stadtzentrum liegen die kleineren, die eher eine typische Fischeratmosphäre bewahren, wie El Portixol, El Molina und Cala Gamba.

Palma is full of terraces that have a good turnover of customers all year round. The Bosch bar, in the heart of the city, at the end of Passeig del Born, is a frequent meeting point for shoppers, workers and tourists who appreciate its sunny terrace as a great place for observing bustling everyday life.

Auf vielen Terrassen in Palma ist das ganze Jahr über ein stetiges Kommen und Gehen zu beobachten. Die Café/Bar Bosch, mitten im Herzen der Stadt am Ende des Passeig del Born gelegen, ist ein beliebter Treffpunkt für die, die zum Shoppen gekommen sind, die in der Nähe arbeiten oder die Touristen, die auf der sonnigen Terrasse ein ideales Plätzchen gefunden haben, um sich von der Lebhaftigkeit des Alltagslebens unterhalten zu lassen.

The Majorcan ensaimada, a spiral-shaped pastry cake much more well-known than another favorite on the island, apricot tart, is a great winner among tourists and visitors.

The old railway line from Palma to Sóller, inaugurated in 1912, is one of the most heavily used tracks on the island. The journey takes an hour and crosses one of the most enchanting parts of the Tramuntana mountain range and then runs onto Port de Sóller.

Das mallorquinische Hefegebäck, die ensaimada, viel bekannter noch als der Aprikosenkuchen, ist eines der häufigsten Mitbringsel der spanischen und ausländischen Besucher.

Die alte Eisenbahn von Palma nach Sóller, die im Jahre 1912 in Betrieb genommen wurde, ist eine der meistbenutzten Schienenverbindungen der Insel. Die Fahrt dauert eine Stunde und führt durch die schönsten Ecken des Gebirgszuges Tramuntana, bis sie schließlich am Meer in Port de Sóller endet.

El Abaco, decorated in an authentic baroque style, is in the historic part of the city of Palma, at close quarters to Sa Llotja.

El Abaco ist im üppigsten Barockstil dekoriert; man findet es in der verwinkelten Altstadt von Palma, in dem Viertel Sa Llotja.

Previous pages:
The project for the Colon restaurant in Porto Colom (Felanitx) is the work of the B&B&W Architecture studio, Sergi Bastides and Wolf Siegfried Wagner. What started out as an old wine cellar was converted into a modern restaurant, always working with the proviso that the pre-existing features – the stone walls and the pillars – were to be integrated and made to stand out. Solid wood beams and a metallic structure cover the ceiling. The arches are finished off with stainless-steel framed glass and a platform of African wood provides the flooring. The general mood of confidence of the interior design is the result of reverentially adapting a traditional space while introducing a 100% vanguardist approach with the new elements.

Auf den vorherigen Seiten:
Das Restaurant Colon in Porto Colom (Felanitx) ist ein Entwurf von B&B&W Estudio de Arquitectura, Sergi Bastides und Wolf Siegfried Wagner. Eine alte Bodega, ein Weinkeller, wurde in dieses moderne Restaurant umgestaltet, dabei wurden die alten Konstruktionselemente wie die gemauerten Ziegelwände und die Pfeiler in das Lokal integriert.
Das Dach besteht aus Holzbalken und einer Metallstruktur; die Bögen sind mit in Edelstahl gerahmten Fenstern verschlossen und der Boden ist mit afrikanischem Holz ausgelegt. Die Räume sind das Ergebnis der behutsamen Umwandlung eines alten Gebäudes, das sich komplett avantgardistisch zeigt.

Inside the restaurant El Ayoun (Ibiza).

Die Speisesäle des Restaurants El Ayoun auf Ibiza.

IGLESIA
PARROQUIAL
DE S FELIU
13

The people of Palma city not only actively take part in the festivities of their own city: they are willing to visit other towns, the Part Forana, to join in the fun of the street parties. One of the most popular pageants is that of the Moors and the Christians held in different towns on the Balearics to commemorate the victories over the Muslims.

Die Palmesanos vergnügen sich nicht nur gerne auf ihren eigenen Stadtfesten, sondern zögern auch nicht, sich in die part forana, d.h. die anderen Ortschaften der Insel aufzumachen, wenn es darum geht, die bekanntesten Fiestas mitzufeiern. Zu den populärsten Festen der Balearen gehören die der Moros i Cristianos (Mauren und Christen), die in verschiedenen Orten verantstaltet werden, um an die Siege über die muselmanischen Besatzer zu erinnern.

In the upper photos you get an idea of the atmosphere during the festival in the town of Pollença. On the t-shirt you can read a few verses written in Majorcan Catalan:

The unfaithful are coming near, guided by a traitor... / Immediately Pollença's few sons gather together bravely... / Joan Mas guides them, he's the bravest of them all... / Immediately the Moors fall back, towards Main street... / Pollença throws them out, with a victorious shout...

Celebrating Moros i Cristians is one of the traditional acts, such as the dance of the cossiers, held during the festival of the patron of Pollença on August 2nd.

This is a popular and traditional dance celebrated in the Majorcan village of Algaida, in which the cossiers jump and dance L'Oferta during the festival of Sant Honorat in winter, and the festival of Sant Jaume in summer. The cossiers are dressed up with green, red and yellow ribbons which stand out brightly against their all-white clothes. On their leggings they wear little bells which jingle to the rhythm of the dance. They carry flowers, handkerchiefs and branches. The ritual symbolizes the victory of the Dama, the lady, over the devil, who always ends up on the ground, trampled under her feet.

Auf diesen Fotos ist das Ambiente des in Pollensa veranstalteten Festes eingefangen. Das T-Shirt beschreibt die Legende in Mallorquin, einem Dialekt der katalanischen Sprache:

Die Ungläubigen nähern sich, geführt von einem Verräter ... / Sofort versammeln sich mutig die wenigen Söhne von Pollença / Joan Mas führt sie an, der tapferste von allen ... / Sogleich weichen die Moren zurück, in der Calle Major (Hauptstraße) ... / Pollença vertreibt sie, mit Siegesgeheul ...

Moros i Cristians wird wie andere Veranstaltungen, z.B. der Tanz der cossiers, während des Stadtfestes zu Ehren der Schutzheiligen von Pollença am 2. August gefeiert.

Der mallorquinische Volkstanz der cossiers ist typisch für den Ort Algaida. Die Tänzer, cossiers, tanzen und hüpfen den Tanz zu Ehren von Sant Honorat im Winter und von Sant Jaume im Sommer. Sie schmücken ihre weiße Kleidung mit bunten Schleifen in Grün, Rot und Gelb. An den Beinen tragen sie kleine Glöckchen, die sich im Rhythmus der Musik bewegen, ebenso wie die Tücher, die Blumen und die Kräutersträußchen. Das Ritual endet mit dem Sieg der Dama über den Teufel, der stets auf dem Boden liegend endet – und sie steht über ihm.

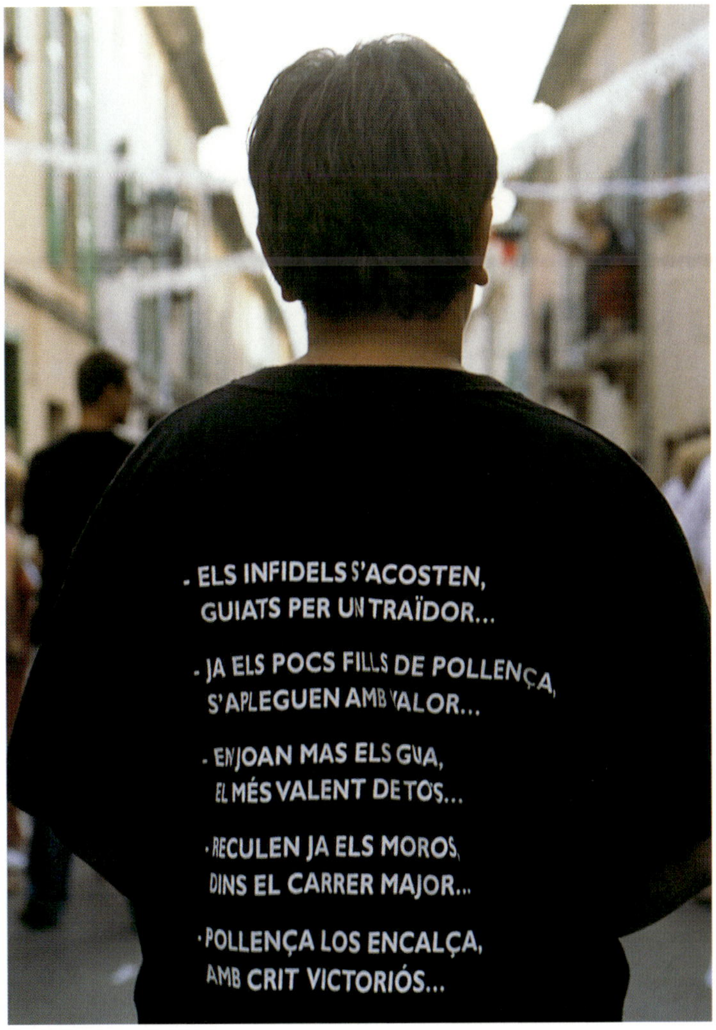

Unicorn is one of the most prestigious decoration shops in the town of Manacor. There is a wide range of furniture in diverse styles and a host of accessories.

Unicorn ist eines der schönsten Dekorations- und Einrichtungsgeschäfte der Stadt Manacor. Es bietet eine große Auswahl Möbel verschiedener Stilrichtungen und dazu passende Accessoires an.

Antoni Muntaner's private house is an example of traditional eighteenth century architecture as well as being a genuine box of surprises. He collects, keeps and sells all types of things which otherwise would be thrown away.

He also sells oriental style furniture, here stored in the old henhouse where the flooring is of worn away little stones (above). In the old stable for the horses, underneath the vaulted ceiling, there is a store of old doors (below).

By the entrance to the home and in the patio, some old furniture, Spanish and foreign amphoras and columns can be seen. In the lower photos we can see some original Stanislas Carrelet vases laid out on a table. In one corner of the living room there is everything from oriental cushions through to rugs of the most diverse origin (right).

Das Haus von Antoni Muntaner im Dorf Santanyí (Mallorca) ist ein Meisterwerk des ländlichen Baustils des 18. Jahrhunderts – und zudem eine wahre Überraschungskiste. Der Eigentümer sammelt, lagert und verkauft alle möglichen Objekte und Materialien vom Sperrmüll und aus Abbruchhäusern.

Zum buntgemischten Angebot gehören auch orientalische Möbel, wie sie im ehemaligen Hühnerstall mit einem Boden aus Kieselsteinen ausgestellt werden (oben). Der alte Pferdestall mit einem Kreuzgewölbe ist das Lager für alte Türen (unten).

Im Eingang des Hauses und zum Innenhof stehen alten Möbel, spanische und importierte Amphoren, Säulen und vieles mehr. Die originellen auf dem Tisch arrangierten Vasen sind von Stanislas Carrelet, und in einer Ecke des Wohnzimmers stapeln sich orientalische Kissen und Teppiche verschiedenster Herkunft (rechts).

Scott's Hotel

This marvellous hotel, situated in Binissalem (Mallorca), displays a facade that exemplifies traditional architecture from Mallorca. Its walls hide spacious salons and rooms, and its interior adopts a romantic a luxurious air that creates a pleasant atmosphere ideal for relaxing. As well as a place of retreat, Scott's ideal location also allows for visitors to discover the beautiful landscapes that surround it.

Dieses einladende Hotel liegt in Binissalem im Inneren der Insel Mallorca. Das Gebäude hat eine Fassade im klassischen mallorquinischen Baustil, hinter der sich großzügige Säle und Zimmer verbergen. Die romantische und luxuriöse Einrichtung verführt zum Entspannen. Scott's ist aber auch ein ideal gelegener Ausgangspunkt, um die zauberhaften Landschaften der Umgebung zu entdecken.

Fundació Pilar i Joan Miró

On the outskirts of the city of Palma, on Cala Major, stand the Fundació Pilar i Joan Miró buildings. They are located on Territori Miró, an idyllic setting with magnificent views over the sea. Inside, an important part of the work of this prolific artist is on display. As a result of Miró's marriage to Pilar Juncosa, native of Mallorca, and his friendship with the Catalan architect Josep Lluís Sert, the Taller Joan Miró (1955) was created. It is the architectural forerunner of the revised Modern Movement and it is considered the starting point of all of Sert's posterior conceptions. Inside the workshop, oil paintings and unfinished canvases revealing Miró's creative process can be contemplated.

The workshop is next to the possessió de Son Boter, a Majorcan country house dating back to the seventeenth century. On the walls there are several pieces of graffiti realized by Miró. The Fundició buildings were constructed thirty years after Sert's workshop. The architect, Rafael Moneo, tried to integrate the "museum" into the site with references to Sert and Miró.

In the upper photo we can see the main façade of the Taller Joan Miró, designed by the architect Josep Lluís Sert.
In the lower photo we can see the Fundació Miró, the work of the architect Rafael Moreno thirty years after the workshop was built.

On the next page we can see a photomontage by the photographer Francesc Cátala-Roca, in which Joan Miró appears in front of some of the graffiti on the walls of Son Boter.

In Cala Major, einem Außenbezirk von Palma, befindet sich die Stiftung Pilar i Joan Miró. Das Ensemble dieser Gebäude - oder auch das Territori Miró - liegt an einem idyllischen Ort mit Blick aufs Meer. Ein bedeutender Teil seines umfangreichen Werkes wird hier ausgestellt. Das Atelier (taller) Joan Mirós ist 1955 dank seiner Ehe mit der Mallorquinerin Pilar Juncosa und seiner Freundschaft mit Josep Lluís Sert entstanden. Das Gebäude ist ein Vorläufer der Erneuerung der Moderne und wird als Ausgangspunkt für das spätere Schaffen des katalanischen Architekten angesehen. Im Atelier kann man verschiedene nicht vollendete Gemälde und Bilder betrachten, die uns den kreativen Prozess Mirós vor Augen führen.

Das Atelier liegt neben dem alten Landgut (possessió) Son Boter aus dem 17. Jahrhundert, an dessen Wänden mehrere Graffitis des Künstlers erhalten sind.

Die Stiftung (Fundació) selbst wurde 30 Jahre nach dem Atelier von Sert von dem spanischen Architekten Rafael Moneo entworfen und versucht sich durch ausdrückliche Bezugnahme auf Sert und Miró in das Ensemble einzugliedern.

Oben sehen wir die Hauptfassade des Taller Joan Miró, das von Josep Lluís Sert gebaut wurde. Die Ansicht unten zeigt einen Teil des Ensembles der Fundació Miró, ein späteres Werk des Architekten Rafael Moneo.

Die Fotomontage von Francesc Cátala-Roca zeigt Joan Miró vor einem seiner Graffitis, die er an die Wände von Son Boter gemalt hat (rechts).

Different views of Miró's workshop and part of his vast number of works.

Verschiedene Ansichten des Ateliers von Joan Miró mit einigen seiner vielen Werke.

The main façade of the possessió de Son Boter.

Die Hauptfassade des Landgutes Son Boter.

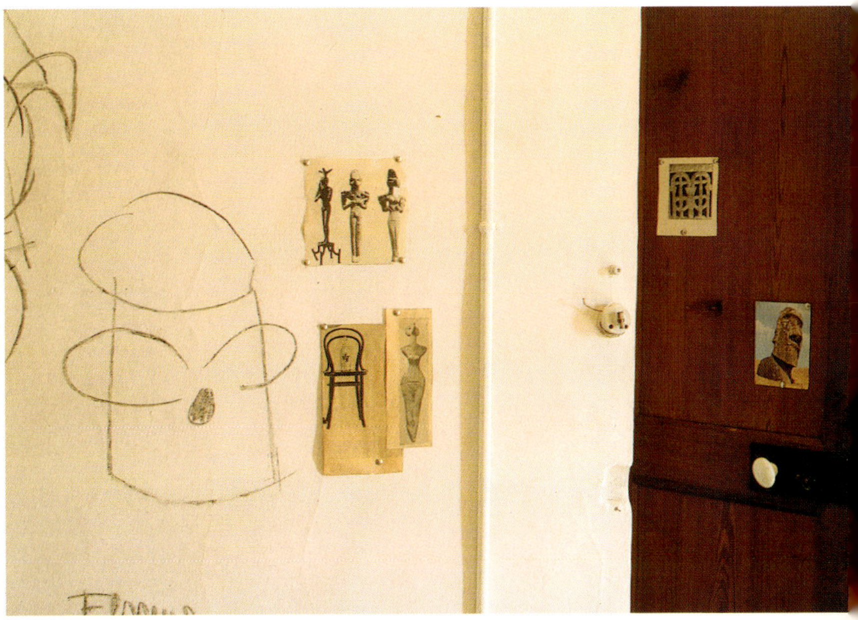

Some of the graffiti and diverse objects found inside the Majorcan country house.

Ein paar Graffitis und verschiedene Objekte, die wir im Inneren des mallorquinischen Landhauses finden.

Very near to Passeig del Born and to Avinguda de Jaume III, in carrer de La Concepció, the Centre de Cultura Sa Nostra is to be found. It was an old eighteenth century palace that was remodeled by the architects Lluís and Jaume García-Ruiz Guasp, with the collaboration of José García-Ruiz Serra. The façade of the building has some still conserved art nouveau details and inside the layout of the old Majorcan patio has remained intact.

The interior garden, a rectangular space, marked off by the octagonal stone pillars rising up into the air, has a water channel and deposit in the middle. Surrounded by lemon trees, it is an ideal place for relaxing, conversing or strolling in a hushed ambience.

Ganz in der Nähe des Passeig del Born und der Avinguda de Jaume III befindet sich in der Calle La Concepció das Kulturzentrum Sa Nostra. Es ist ein alter Palast aus dem 18. Jahrhundert, der von den Architekten Lluís und Jaume García-Ruiz Guasp unter Mitarbeit von José García-Ruiz Serra umgebaut wurde. An der Fassade sind noch einige der erhaltenen Jugendstil-Details zu sehen. Auch der alte mallorquinischen Innenhof konnte bewahrt werden.

Der zum Himmel offene rechteckige Garten im Inneren, wird von achteckigen Holzsäulen und Zitronenbäumen eingerahmt. Ein kleiner Kanal und eine gemauerte Zisterne gehören dazu. Es ist das ideale Plätzchen, um sich auszuruhen, sich zu unterhalten oder in dem ruhigen und verschwiegenen Ambiente zu lustwandeln.

Previous page:
In this photo of the entrance you can see how the arches, sustained by columns with Ionic volutes, lead into the large patio. The staircase has a wrought iron banister. The fount against the wall, right next to the staircase, stands out. The geometric pattern on the floor is composed of small pebbles worn smooth by the action of the sea.

Vorherige Seite:
Im Eingang zum Palast werden majestätische Bögen von Säulen mit ionischen Voluten getragen und öffnen sich zu einem weitläufigen patio. Eine Treppe mit einem schmiedeeisernen Gitter steigt vom Eingang empor. An der Wand des ersten Treppenlaufs fällt ein kleines Stein-Waschbecken auf. Auf dem Fußboden zeichnen runde Kiesel über den gesamten Innenhof geometrische Muster.

The garden of the Centro de Cultura Sa Nostra is next to a quiet café and restaurant with a terrace where you can observe the everyday life of ordinary people.

The cultural center was restored respecting the building's history and opened up to the public for a host of uses. On its three floors there are exposition rooms for contemporary art, a modern auditorium, a bookshop and a video center specializing in art with a strong emphasis on the Balearic Islands. Finally, there is an Image and Communication Center and a zone reserved for administration.

Vom Garten des Centro de Cultura Sa Nostra gelangt man in ein ruhiges Café/Restaurant mit einer großen Terrasse, von der man ein paar Blicke auf das nächstgelegene städtische Umfeld erhaschen kann.

Das Kulturzentrum wurde unter Berücksichtigung der Vergangenheit des Gebäudes saniert und hat sich zu einer modernen Mehrzweckeinrichtung entwickelt. Über die drei Stockwerke verteilen sich mehrere Ausstellungssäle für zeitgenössische Kunst, ein modernes Auditorium, eine auf Kunst spezialisierte Buchhandlung sowie eine Videothek, deren Schwerpunktthema die Balearen sind. Außerdem sind im Zentrum ein Film- und Kommunikationszentrum sowie der Verwaltungsbereich untergebracht.

Designer Apartment

This flat, situated very near to Palma, is the result of a project by B&B Estudio de Arquitectura, Sergi Bastides. They adapted an old blacksmith's forge, which had occupied a building of two floors, turning the ground floor into an architect's office and the upper floor into living quarters.

The home has a floor space of two hundred square meters, all the traditional rooms being generously sized. The walls are not conventional: the living room, the kitchen, and other rooms, are separated by aluminum partitions and others not reaching up to the ceiling.

The living room, conceived like a metallic self-contained unit, is thermally and acoustically isolated. The beams, painted white in both the living room and the bathroom - where they follow the slope of the roof - do not go unnoticed. The flooring is polished concrete livened up by bright hand-woven carpets.

The decoration is good taste hotchpotch: an anarchic and very personal mixture playing off different styles of furniture from diverse epochs so as to create original ambiences around the flat.

The main façade of this old forge, with all the hallmarks of the late nineteenth and early twentieth centuries, hides away the restoration of the interior, now totally modernized.

This living area design is based on the boundaries created by the aluminum partitions. Relaxation and rest are provided by the red leather sofa, its classic look and modern lines set off against different styles of the armchairs.

Designer Apartment

Diese Wohnung ganz in der Nähe von Palma wurde von B&B Estudio de Arquitectura, Sergi Bastides, gestaltet. In diesem zweistöckigen Manufaktur-Gebäude, einer alten Schmiede, wurde das Erdgeschoss in ein Architekturbüro und die darüber liegende Etage in die dazugehörige Wohnung umgebaut.

Auf dem weitläufigen Grundriss von 200m² verteilen sich die herkömmlichen Wohnräume, auffällig sind jedoch die Raumteiler in einigen Bereichen, wie beispielsweise im Wohnzimmer oder in der Küche. Einige sind mit Aluminium verkleidet oder bilden Trennwände, die nicht bis zur Decke reichen.

Das Wohnzimmer, wie eine Blechkiste geplant, hat eine spezielle Wärme- und Schallisolierung. Die weiß gestrichenen Deckenbalken verlaufen im Bad parallel zur Dachschräge. Im gesamten Haus ist der Fußboden aus poliertem Beton, fröhliche Kelims sorgen für Farbtupfer.

Die Einrichtung dieser Wohnung spiegelt einen leicht anarchischen und sehr persönlichen Geschmack wider: Möbel verschiedenster Stile und Epochen wurden zu einem abwechslungsreichen Ambiente kombiniert.

Die Hauptfassade dieses Manufaktur-Gebäudes mit ihrer Gestaltungsform von Ende des 19. und Anfang des 20. Jahrhunderts lässt nicht erahnen, dass sich dahinter ein moderner und avantgardistischer Umbau befindet.

Das Wohnzimmer, von Aluminiumwänden eingefasst, wurde mit einem leuchtend roten Ledersofa in klassisch moderner Linie sowie Sesseln verschiedener Stilrichtungen eingerichtet.

Another way of separating two spaces is by using a bookcase in the middle of which there is an opening through into the next room. Against the far wall an elegant cupboard can be seen.

Eine andere Möglichkeit, die verschiedenen Bereiche voneinander zu teilen, stellt dieses Bücherregal dar, das über dem Türrahmen verbunden ist und den Vitrinenschrank im Hintergrund einrahmt.

The kitchen´s partition stops short of the ceiling. Behind lies an L-shaped room. The table has a wood top and iron legs; the seating is taken care of by the recurring chairs, commonly associated with film directors.

Die Küchenwand stößt nicht bis an die Decke; dahinter liegt ein weiterer L-förmiger Raum. Der Küchentisch besteht aus einer Holzplatte mit einem Metallgestell, und die bequemen Regie-Stühle beschwören die Atmosphäre Hollywoods.

This view of the living room, which leads on into the bedrooms, highlights a painting by Francesc Roca, placed next to the sofas. In the upper photo we can see a close up of the sofa design: it is made of red leather and aluminum. Attached to the back of it there are two spotlights.

Diese Ansicht des Wohnzimmers lenkt den Blick auf ein Werk des Malers Francesc Roca, das über dem Sofa aufgehängt wurde. Von hier gelangt man in eines der Schlafzimmer. Der Reiz des Sofas liegt in der Kombination von Aluminium mit dem knalligen Leder; zwei kleine Leselampen sind an der Rückseite befestigt.

In the master bedroom the decoration is Moroccan all round the room, the headboard of the bed being especially noteworthy.

The bathroom, decorated with matt stuccowork, is just off the master bedroom. The design of the bathroom unit and taps is by the company Aqua Aquae.

Im Haupt-Schlafzimmer hat man sich für eine Dekoration im marokkanischen Stil entschieden: Das Kopfteil des Bettes dominiert den Raum.

Das matt verputzte Badezimmer hat direkten Zugang zum Schlafzimmer. Das Waschbecken und die Armaturen sind von der Firma Aqua Aquae.

Painter's Home and Studio

The home of artist Francesc Roca, located in a building in the center of the village of Artà, has the conventional internal layout of a city home. However, the plus side is that the ambience and surroundings, above all the patio, are as tranquil as anything to be found in a little town.

The patio, adorned with flowerbeds and flowerpots, retains its intimacy thanks to the high walls. From it one can access directly into the kitchen and the rooms on the ground floor of the house.

Inside the house there are two clearly differentiated spaces: the living quarters on the first two floors and the workshop and general creative area upstairs in the loft. Some of the painter's works are distributed around the residence, and others - work in progress - are to be found in the workshop.

The bedrooms are on the first floor, along with a terrace joined to the patio by means of a staircase.

Wood beams run across the ceiling in the classic style of this type of house. The flooring is concrete painted in a cream color.

In the dining room attention is focused on one of the artist's works. Around a wood table fitted with handy drawers, there are wicker chairs, original for the wood design of the seat and back.

Haus und Atelier eines Malers

Die Wohnung des Künstlers Francesc Roca befindet sich in einem Haus im Zentrum des Ortes Artà und entspricht von ihrer Innengestaltung her einer typischen Stadtwohnung. Im kleinen Innenhof jedoch ist die Atmosphäre so entspannt und ruhig, dass man eher meint, auf dem Dorf zu sein.

Der mit einigen niedrigen Pflanzen und Blumenkübeln geschmückte Innenhof bewahrt dank seiner hohen Mauern eine private und zurückgezogene Atmosphäre. Man betritt ihn über die Küche oder das Wohnzimmer im Erdgeschoss des Hauses.

Der Innenraum teilt sich in zwei Bereiche: die Wohnung als solche, die sich über die beiden unteren Geschosse erstreckt, und das Atelier mit der Werkstatt in den alten Dachkammern. Einige Werke des Malers sind über die Wohnung verteilt; andere, die noch mitten im kreativen Prozess stecken, stehen im Atelier bereit. An die erste Etage, wo sich die Schlafzimmer befinden, schließt sich auch eine Terrasse an, die über eine Treppe mit dem Innenhof verbunden ist.

Die Decken innen wurden mit den für die regionale Architektur charakteristischen Holzbalken gestaltet, und der Fußboden im gesamten Haus ist lasierter in einem Crème-Ton gestrichener Zement.

Die Einrichtung des Esszimmers besteht aus einem Holztisch mit praktischen Schubladen und einer handvoll Stühlen aus Korbweide, die einen originell gestalteten Holzabschluss haben. Es ist jedoch das Kunstwerk des Eigentümers, dass die gesamte Aufmerksamkeit auf sich zieht.

In the kitchen the unpolished wall covering of mares stone, above a run of standard tiles, gives a country feel to the room. A sliding glass door, with an aluminum frame, leads out to the rear patio.

Die Küchenwand mit dem unbehandelten Kalkstein (marès) oberhalb der Keramikfliesen verleiht dem Raum ein rustikales und fröhliches Aussehen. Von hier gelangt man über eine doppelte Glastür mit Aluminiumrahmen in den hinter dem Haus gelegenen kleinen Hof.

J. BENNASSAR
GALERIA MARIETA GUAL

Upstairs, as the traditional Majorcan loft is generously sized it has been set aside as a work area and is great for toiling away on large paintings. On some of the walls the raw stone has been left untouched while in other zones it has been mortared over and painted white.

Der klassische mallorquinische porxo, im allgemeinen als Lager genutzt, ist dem Atelier vorbehalten. Der großzügige Raum erlaubt es, Gemälde in ungewöhnlichen Formaten zu bearbeiten. Die ehemaligen Dachkammern bewahren an einigen Stellen den unbehandelten Stein, während andere Abschnitte verputzt und weiß gestrichen wurden.

The old pigeon loft was on the first floor. The reed roof and original walls have been conserved. The flooring has been covered with matting made of coconut fibers.

Im ersten Stock befand sich ein alter Taubenschlag. Heute sind noch das mit Rohrgeflecht gedeckte Dach und die Mauern aus dem Kalkstein marès vorhanden. Für den Fußboden wählte man diesen derben Kokosbelag.

The rear patio is covered by stone slabs to form an extension of the living area which enables the inhabitants to enjoy pleasant outdoor meals.

Der Hof hinter dem Haus ist mit Steinplatten ausgelegt und verlängert den Wohnraum nach draußen, so dass man gemütlich die Mahlzeiten im Freien genießen kann.

The main façade of the house is typical of the zone. From the artist's studio there is a view over the neighboring houses.

Die Frontseite des Hauses, im typischen Stil des Inselinneren, und der Blick über die Dächer der angrenzenden Häuser, wie man ihn vom Atelier aus hat.

Enchanted Garden

A pathway through the garden leads up to the main façade with its two doors going into the ground floor.

The possibility of finding a house like this in Palma is one in a million. Located in the old quarter of the city, the remit to redevelop this house was entrusted to Antonio Obrador and his office Estudio Denario Arquitectura.

The home occupies all of the ground floor of an old L-shaped building surrounded by an incredible garden with enormous palm trees and a modern swimming pool. On both sides there are porches, one of them closed off with giant doors, while the other is totally open and held up by stone columns and fine iron work. A channel for the water runs from the first porch to the pool.

Although the library and the living room -which together with the dining room enjoy a view of the garden- have been given priority, all the rooms are large. As well as the garden, there is also an interior patio.

The sturdiness of the thick walls is evident. The quality of the doors matches the fine marquetry inlaid on them. Wood beams run across the ceiling and the flooring is of polished limestone.

The porch, in front of a pond with water lilies and papyrus, can be closed off by the sliding doors during the winter months without sacrificing any natural light and the warmth of the sun coming through the glass, just as if one were outside.

Verzauberter Garten

Die Chancen so ein Haus in Palma zu finden, stehen eins zu einer Million. Die in der Altstadt gelegene Villa ist ein Sanierungsprojekt von Antonio Obrador und seinem Büro Estudio Denario Arquitectura.

Die Wohnung nimmt das gesamte Erdgeschoss eines alten L-förmigen Gebäudes ein, das sich um einen unglaublichen Garten mit hohen, alten Palmen und einen avantgardistischen Swimming Pool schmiegt. Auf beiden Seiten öffnen sich Veranden. Die eine ist mit großen gläsernen Schiebetüren verschlossen – von hier zieht sich ein Kanal als klare Achse bis zum Pool –, und die andere mit steinernen Pfeilern und filigranen Eisensäulen ist offen.

Die Grundflächen der verschiedenen Zimmer sind großzügig, aber der Bibliothek und dem Wohnzimmer wurden Priorität eingeräumt. Diese beiden Räume sowie das Esszimmer haben Blick auf den Garten. Im Inneren des Hauses gibt es außerdem noch einen Innenhof.

Die dicken Mauern verdeutlichen ihre solide Bauweise, und die Schwere der Türen passt gut zu den feinen Intarsienarbeiten. Die Decken bestehen aus den alten Holzbalken und die Böden sind mit poliertem Kalkstein ausgelegt.

Die Hauptfassade, zu der man über einen begrünten Weg gelangt, öffnet sich mit zwei Toren zum Erdgeschoss.

Die Veranda, gegenüber einem Gartenteich mit Wasserlilien und Papyrus, wird in den Wintermonaten mit Schiebetüren verschlossen, ohne dadurch Helligkeit und Sonnenwärme einzubüßen, die durch die großen Scheiben eindringt und den angenehmen Eindruck vermittelt, man befände sich im Freien.

Wood was considered to be the best material for this outstanding library, beams across the ceiling, shelving on the walls and even above the hearth. It adds a rectilinear aspect to the walls and makes the room feel warm and cozy. The comfortable sofas are arranged besides little tables and four lamps in the same style.

Holz wurde als Material für diese eindrucksvolle Bibliothek gewählt, die sich in einer einzigen Linie an den Wänden entlangstreckt, sogar über dem Kaminsims, und eine warme und gemütliche Atmosphäre vermittelt. Die einladenden Sofas wurden mit verschiedenen Beistelltischen arrangiert, auf denen vier identische Lampen stehen.

The works of art and the paintings by contemporary artists are prominent in most of the rooms. The living room has a decorative style identical to that of the library: elegant, classic and refined, exuding good taste. The Art work is by Agustí Puig and Joaquín Torrens Lladó.

In den meisten Räumen fallen die Kunstwerke und Gemälde zeitgenössischer Künstler auf. Das Wohnzimmer ist im gleichen Stil wie die Bibliothek eingerichtet: elegant, klassisch und raffiniert verrät es einen exquisiten Geschmack. Die Gemälde sind von Agustí Puig und Joaquín Torrens Lladó.

The master bedroom is dominated by the colonial style bed and the two antique bedside tables. The room accesses directly into the main bathroom originally fitted out in black and white marble. Everything is personalized twice over: there are two showers and two wash basins but no bathtub. The curved arches and vaulted ceiling give the room the ambience of a Turkish bath.

The guests' bathroom is just as original in its design: the yellow marble, its veins clearly visible, sets the tone.

Das Elternschlafzimmer wurde mit diesem Bett im Kolonialstil und zwei antiken Nachttischchen eingerichtet. Es ist direkt mit dem größten Badezimmer verbunden, das aus weißem und schwarzen Marmor besteht und ein originelles Design hat. Die Bereiche wurden auf die Personen zugeschnitten: zwei Duschen und zwei Waschbecken, für die die Badewanne geopfert wurde. Die geschwungene Form der Bögen und des Gewölbes erinnern an ein türkisches Bad.

Das Gästebad wurde ebenfalls mit Einfallsreichtum gestaltet: aus in Gelbtönen gemasertem Marmor.

Houses in the historic part of the city tend to be lacking in daylight and therefore the quality of light in this one is really a privilege. The corridor leading to the library has blunt arched windows along it which break down the barrier between the inside and the garden. On the walls we can contemplate part of the art collection.

Die Helligkeit dieses Hauses, das mitten in der Altstadt von Palma liegt, ist ein außergewöhnliches Privileg. In diesem breiten Korridor, der zur Bibliothek führt, öffnen sich große Fenster mit Rundbögen zum Garten und überwinden so die Grenze zwischen drinnen und draußen. An den Wänden kann man einen Teil der Kunstsammlung betrachten.

The garden has been conceived more in line with the Hispano-Moorish tradition than the European, not only because of its delicate and lovingly cared for look but also because of some of the architectural elements such as the pavilion on the other side of the pool and the pillars by its door.

Die Anlage des Gartens folgt eher einem spanisch-arabischen Schema als einem europäischen und wird nicht nur in seiner feinen und gepflegten Schönheit sichtbar, sondern auch in einigen Elementen der Architektur, wie dem Pavillon im Hintergrund und den Säulen, die seine Eingangstür einrahmen.

This influence is also visible in the water channel that leads one's eye from the glass windows of the porch to the swimming pool. Arab culture always revered water and incorporated it into the architecture.

Auch der kleine Kanal, der eine gerade Linie von der verglasten Veranda zu einem der Eckpunkte des Swimming Pools zieht, erinnert an diesen Stil. Der Pool wurde in der Art eines offenen Sammelbrunnens, wie er in der arabischen Kultur vorkommt, gestaltet.

Inspiring Views

Mallorca is home to many artists born here. However, many others come here from other regions of Spain and from abroad, attracted to these Mediterranean islands not only by the luminosity but also by the quality of life. The artist Dolores Sampol chose to set up her studio and home in the historic part of the city of Palma.

From the intimacy of her own home the painter can look out at the sublime cathedral, la Seu de Palma. It is a fantastic view to have beyond the canvas when painting.

The duplex is part of a city building. Throughout all the home the darkened wood beams have been conserved. By the entrance a staircase leads up to the studio. The living room has a little balcony with outside vistas.

On the upper floor there is a large space for working. It opens up onto a grand terrace sheltered from the sun by an awning. From here the view of the cathedral is spectacular.

The layout of the living room was decided on with the bookshelves very much in mind. The intense light coming in from the balcony, the peacefulness and the comfortable sofas together all make this an ideal place for resting or reading.

Inspirierende Aussicht

Mallorca ist die Wiege vieler lokaler Künstler. Aber ebenso haben spanische und internationale Künstler die Insel zu ihrer Wahlheimat erklärt und diese Mittelmeerinsel nicht nur wegen des besonderen Lichts, sondern auch wegen ihrer Lebensqualität gewählt. Die Künstlerin Dolores Sampol hat in der Altstadt von Palma ihren Wohnsitz und ihr Atelier eingerichtet.

In der Zurückgezogenheit ihrer Wohnung überrascht der schöne und rare Blick auf die Kathedrale, la Seu. Unterm Dach steht der Malerin außerdem ein fantastischer Raum für ihr kreatives Arbeiten mit Leinwänden zur Verfügung.

Die Wohnung, in einem hübschen Stadthaus gelegen, erstreckt sich über zwei Geschosse und hat noch die alten Decken mit den dunkel gewordenen Holzbalken. Vom Eingang aus führt eine Treppe nach oben ins Atelier und eine andere ins Wohnzimmer, dem ein kleiner Balkon mit Blick nach draußen vorgelagert ist.

Unterm Dach richtete die Künstlerin ihren Arbeitsplatz ein, der direkt mit der großen Terrasse verbunden ist. Schutz vor der Sonne bietet eine dicke Segeltuch-Plane. Von hier hat man einen spektakulären Blick auf die Kathedrale.

Das Bücherregal rahmt die Einrichtung des Wohnzimmers ein. Dank des Lichts, das vom Balkon hereinströmt, der Ruhe und den gemütlichen Sofas ist dies ein ideales Plätzchen, um zu lesen oder auszuruhen.

In the dining room a classic wood table has been paired off with the more contemporary design of the aluminum chairs. Some paintings of the different artist's are on the wall. In the kitchen, too, more of her art collection can be admired as one sits at the table. A nearly unnoticeable glass door which isolates off the upper floor from the rest of the home (left).

Im Esszimmer spielt dieses Arrangement eines klassischen Holztisches mit modernen Aluminiumstühlen die Hauptrolle. An der Wand hängen einige Werke verschiedener Künstler. Auch die Küche, in der ein Esstisch steht, dient als Hintergrund für einen Teil der Kunstsammlung. Mit einer nahezu unsichtbaren Glastür kann man den Zugang zur oberen Etage verschließen und sie so vom Rest der Wohnung trennen (links).

The best place for feasting one's eyes on the extraordinary view is, beyond a shadow of a doubt, this terrace. Few people are lucky enough to be able to view the cathedral from this vantage point, let alone lunch or dine leisurely glancing up from their plate every now and then. At night the Seu and the city ramparts are lit up. You can just imagine how beautiful it looks.

Nur wenige kommen in den Genuss dieser Perspektive auf la Seu von Palma, und noch weniger können jeden Tag mit ihr im Blick zu Mittag oder zu Abend essen. Nachts ist die Kathedrale beleuchtet, genau wie die alte Stadtmauer, der Rest bleibt der eigenen Fantasie überlassen ...

The big studio is used to store the painter's work that will later be shipped off to her expositions. The size of the windows means that daylight is more than adequate for her creative work. The room, stripped of decoration, makes no concession to resting. Any break from the canvas should be taken by simply stepping out onto the fantastic open-air terrace (left).

Das geräumige Atelier dient auch als Lager für die Gemälde und Arbeiten der Künstlerin, die zu verschiedenen Ausstellungen durch die Welt geschickt werden. Dank der großen Fenster kann sie bei natürlichem Licht arbeiten, was für den kreativen Prozess sehr wichtig ist. Der Raum selbst, ohne jegliche Dekoration, lädt nicht gerade zum Ausruhen ein. Pausieren kann man stattdessen auf der wunderbaren Terrasse draußen, die direkt vom Atelier zugänglich ist (links).

Living in the Countryside

Leben auf dem Land

Living in the Countryside

In Mallorca there is an expression, of which there is no exact equivalent in Spanish, used to refer to the people not born in Palma, the island's capital, and therefore different to those born in this city. On the island the locals say that a person is either from the capital, Palma, or one is from the part forana – "the foreign part" – that is from anywhere else on the island. Some residents of the city of Palma, descendents of the gentry or the upper classes, also have a country home where they spend the weekends, thereby dividing their time between the two different ambiences. However, outside the city the locals used to live off the land, seven days a week, working in the fields or dedicated to the livestock industry and this marked their personality.

The tranquil rural pace of life was interrupted when the tourist sector took off. The big changes that have made an impact on the islands since then have not yet fed completely through to the majority of villages and hamlets in the interior, nor to the country houses dotted around. However, in the urban areas, which have grown in size, and along the coasts, where land available for construction is beginning to run out, the changes have made themselves felt as urbanizations have sprung up.

The building of country homes dates back to the middle ages. The oldest ones were originally Muslim farmsteads but after the Catalans conquered the isles in 1229 an effort was made to permanently populate the rural areas and to give a boast to the agrarian economy by setting up villages with their own churches. The plan of these churches, intended to aid in the repopulating of the land and in the establishment of a centralized order, was very simple: there was just one nave covered by an arched wooden roof. In contrast, the convents, which were not principally instruments for "reclaiming land" were more evolved in their architectural design: there was a polygonal presbytery, chapels between the buttresses and either a flat wooden roof or cross ribbed arches. This model was used in the construction of the palatine chapels like the Trinitat de la Seu.

Farmhouses and other homes in the villages were constructed thinking first in the needs of life in the country. It must be remembered that there are important differences in the architectural features of the homes on the three islands and the explanations given here are primarily applicable to Mallorca.

Around the vilas (villages) possessions were built. These were basically homes for the agricultural workers and were supplemented by many barracas, a lower class of home half-way between a hut and a cottage which were often shared with the animals. Barracas were constructed out of stone without using mortar – this old technique was known as dry wall building and was also used for the walls between the properties, known as marges.

Leben auf dem Land

Auf Mallorca wird für den Unterschied, auf dem Lande oder in der Stadt geboren worden zu sein, ein Ausdruck verwendet, für den es in der spanischen Sprache keine Übersetzung gibt. Hier ist man entweder aus der Hauptstadt, aus Palma, oder man kommt von der part forana, das heißt, von irgendwoher auf der Insel. Manche Einwohner Palmas, aus dem Adel oder aus wohlhabenden Kreisen, hatten ein Gut (possessió) auf dem Lande, wo sie die Wochenenden verbrachten und so ihre Zeit zwischen beiden Lebensräumen teilten. Die Bevölkerung außerhalb der Stadt lebte von der bäuerlichen Arbeit, d.h. Landwirtschaft und Viehzucht.

Diese Situation veränderte sich mit dem Aufblühen des Fremdenverkehrs völlig. Die großen Umwälzungen, die sich von diesem Moment an auf den Inseln abspielten, sind bis jetzt noch nicht in den Großteil der Dörfer im Inland und auch nicht bis in die Landhäuser gedrungen, obwohl die Stadtzentren deutlich angewachsen sind und der Baugrund entlang der Küstengebiete durch das lange Zeit unkontrollierte Wuchern von Siedlungen jeglicher Art langsam knapp wird.

Die ländlichen Bauten entwickelten sich ab dem Mittelalter. Die ältesten gehen auf muselmanische Landgüter zurück; nach der Eroberung durch Katalonien (1229) wurde jedoch versucht, die Bevölkerung dauerhaft auf dem Land anzusiedeln und der Wirtschaft durch die Gründung von Dörfern und den dazugehörigen Kirchen Auftrieb zu geben. Der Grundriss dieser sogenannten Wiederbevölkerungs-Kirchen war denkbar einfach: ein einziges, mit Holz abgedecktes und von Rundbögen getragenes Schiff. Im Gegensatz dazu wies die Architektur der Konvente schon weiterentwickelte Formen auf: einen vieleckigen Chorraum, Kapellen zwischen den Bogenpfeilern und ein flaches Dach aus Holz oder eine Konstruktion aus Kreuzbögen. Dieses Modell findet man in den Palastkapellen, wie zum Beispiel der Kapelle Trinitat de la Seu.

Die Bauernhöfe und die Häuser der Dörfer wurden in einer sehr ähnlichen Bauweise errichtet, stets an die Bedürfnisse des Lebens auf dem Lande angepasst. In diesem Zusammenhang sollte darauf hingewiesen werden, dass es zwischen den Inseln bedeutende Unterschiede in der Konstruktionsweise gibt und dass hier in erster Linie von Mallorca die Rede ist.

The possessió, architecturally more complicated than a simple farmhouse, was the center point of a group of buildings organized around the patio where the community tasks were carried out. It consisted of a house for the land owners, often with its own small chapel, a house for the man and wife entrusted with running farming matters and then a series of rooms for storing the harvest of wheat and barley and for sheltering the livestock, principally sheep, goats and pigs. All of these farms had cellars, tanks, reservoirs and wells. In addition, some of them had a tafona - a grinding wheel for oil - and a cellar for oil and wine, a windmill, a waterwheel and the typical round threshing floor.

Around the farms the typical crops of the Mediterranean were sown and are still cultivated today. There are almond trees in Mallorca and Ibiza. Some parts of Mallorca, Binissalem, Consell and Santa Maria, were traditional vine growing areas but today they are in decline. Olives, too, were grown but now in the twenty first century they are hardly noticeable. On the Pitiusas islands - the name given by the Romans to Ibiza and Formentera - there are fig trees, above all on Formentera. Cereal production, another sector on the wane, is concentrated on Mallorca, concretely in Es Pla, Manacor and Llucmajor. Finally, the most common irrigation crops are garden produce, potatoes and citrus fruits in the valley of Sóller.

One characteristic of country life gives a lot away about how things used to be on the islands. Country folk would sleep with the door left unlocked, but distrust has crept into even the most isolated regions as the population has increased. In small villages new arrivals still arouse curiosity, and even a slight stand-off attitude. Nobody is accepted until more is known about them. Traditional values still hold sway in these domains and public opinion, or the village opinion, believes it has the right to judge the behavior of other people, especially new-comers, as if one's own morality was superior.

To understand this it is necessary to go back two or three generations when hamlets were quite cut off and foreigners were hardly ever seen. Ethical codes - basically traditional catholic ones - became quite deeply rooted and it is only tourism which has gradually changed society, bringing with it economic prosperity but also spoiling many harmonious aspects of a hamlet. It has been difficult for older people to feel at ease with this "progress".

Um die Dörfer (vilas) herum verteilten sich die Landgüter, Bauernhäuser und unzählige Baracken, in denen oft Menschen und Tiere unter demselben Dach zusammenlebten. Die Baracken wurden aus Natursteinen ohne Mörtel gemäss der alten Trockenmauer-Technik gebaut, die auch heute noch für die Mauern verwendet wird, die die Grundstücke voneinander abgrenzen.

Die possessió, ein größeres Bauwerk als das Bauernhaus, gruppiert mehrere Gebäude um einen zentralen Hof (clastra) herum, wo die gemeinschaftlichen Aufgaben erledigt wurden. Dieser Komplex besteht aus dem Herrenhaus, zu dem häufig auch eine kleine Kapelle gehört; aus dem Haus der Wirtschafter, die sich um Landwirtschaft und Viehzucht kümmerten, und einer Reihe Nebengebäude für die Lagerung von landwirtschaftlichen Produkten (Weizen, Hafer ...) und die Unterbringung der Tiere (hauptsächlich Schafe, Ziegen und Schweine). Dazu gehörten Zisternen, Brunnen, Sammelbecken für Regenwasser und gemauerte Speicher. Manchmal findet man auch die Ölpresse tafona oder den celler für die Wein-Herstellung, Wind- und Wassermühlen sowie die typische runde Tenne zum Dreschen.

Um die ländlichen Häuser herum wurden die charakteristischen Bäume und Pflanzen der Mittelmeer-Landschaft angebaut: der Mandelbaum auf Mallorca und Ibiza; Weinberge, wenn auch diese beständig abnehmen, in den Anbaugebieten von Mallorca wie Binissalem, Consell oder Santa María sowie der Olivenbaum, der heute fast bedeutungslos ist. Auf den Pitiusas stößt man auch auf Feigenbäume, vor allem auf der Insel Formentera. Der Anbau von Getreide, ebenfalls rückgängig, konzentriert sich auf die mallorquinischen Gemeinden Es Pla, Manacor und Llucmajor. In Gegenden mit Bewässerungssystemen schließlich werden Gemüse, Kartoffeln und Zitrusfrüchte angebaut, letztere insbesondere im Tal von Sóller.

Ein interessanter Aspekt betrifft den Charakter der ländlichen Bevölkerung. Bis vor kurzem lebten und schliefen die Bauern mit unverschlossenen Türen. Das Vertrauen ist jedoch ein Element, das infolge der konstanten Bevölkerungszunahme und der steigenden Unsicherheit in der engsten Umgebung langsam verschwindet. In den kleinen Dörfern ist die Neugier auf einen neuen Einwohner noch immer groß; er ist auch erst wirklich aufgenommen, wenn alle ihn kennen. An diesen Orten gelten die traditionellen Werte unverändert. Man bewahrt so etwas wie ein Volksgewissen, das sich darauf beschränkt, fremdes Verhalten anhand einer sogenannten Moral zu beurteilen.

Um dieses Verhalten zu verstehen, braucht man nur zwei oder drei Generationen zurückzugehen in eine Zeit, in der die Dörfer mehr oder weniger isoliert und Fremde selten waren. Man muss berücksichtigen, dass die Traditionen, besonders diejenigen, die sich auf die Moral beziehen, in den kleinen Dörfern tiefer verwurzelt sind und dass der Wechsel von einer ländlichen Gesellschaft zu einer Gesellschaft, die hauptsächlich vom Tourismus lebt, in den letzten dreißig Jahren bedeutende soziale Umwandlungen mit sich gebracht hat, die ältere Leute nur schwer akzeptieren können.

Country Landscapes

Insel-Landschaften

Country Landscapes

These green fields and the numerous windmills with their sails gently rotating against the blue, luminous afternoon sky could fill pages and the beholder would not grow tired of admiring their beauty. They are sights that stay with us in the memory, reminding us of these alluring landscapes.

Another idyllic scene so often captured by the camera is that of almond trees in their finest moment as they blossom. At this time of year the islands are full of pure colors which anticipate the change of season. Spring is impatient to show off its range of bright colors bathed by the Mediterranean sun. Every heart cheering shade of yellow will appear, the ephemeral red of the poppies in the fields, and the blues and violets of the wild flowers growing along the hedges as the earth comes to life.

And to finish this picturesque country landscape, do not forget the flocks of sheep and goats that leisurely graze around the fields and on the verges. When the sun is at its hottest they form silent groups in the shade of a fig tree or a carob tree. Sometime the branches of these trees are held open with stakes to extend the shadow so that all the flock can find respite under this improvised porch.

One of the most serene and peaceful villages on Mallorca is Valldemossa on the Serra de Tramuntana. Surrounded by mountains, it is built on a hillside with holding walls, called marges in Mallorquin. Its sloping streets are full of balconies and doorways decorated with flowers, turning it into a little paradise, modest but real. The writer George Sands and her lover, the composer Chopin, passed the winter of 1838–39 in the Cartoixa de Valldemossa. Originally la Cartoixa was to be a royal palace but it ended up as a monastery after it was inhabited by Carthusian monks in 1399. Nearby the Palau del Rei Sanxo and the church of Sant Bartomeu are also worth visiting.

Insel-Landschaften

Diese grüne Erde mit ihren unzähligen Windmühlen, die sich mit ihren Flügeln vom blauen, leuchtenden Himmel abheben, könnten mit ihren Bildern Seiten um Seiten eines Buches füllen, ohne dass man müde würde, sie zu betrachten. Diese Bilder leben in unserem Gedächtnis und in der Erinnerung an diese wunderschöne Landschaft fort.

Ein anderer unvergesslicher Eindruck dieser idyllischen Landschaft sind die Mandelbäume während ihres prächtigsten Augenblicks: ihrer Blüte. In dieser Zeit kleiden sich die Inseln in pure Farben, die den Wechsel der Jahreszeiten erahnen lassen. Der Frühling, der ungeduldig darauf wartet, mit seinen leuchtenden, hellen Tönen zu prahlen, die ohne Zweifel seine herrliche Gestalt im Glanz des mediterranen Lichtes noch verschönern. Gelb in allen Schattierungen erfreut das Herz, rote Felder mit zarten Mohnblumen, blaue und violette Töne, unzählige verschiedene Blumenarten vermischen sich auf den Feldern für das prunkvolle Gewand des Frühlings.

Zur Vervollständigung dieses ländlichen Stillebens kann man auch ein ganz alltägliches Bild erwähnen, nämlich die Schafe und Ziegen, die träge auf den Feldern herumwandern und die, wenn die Sonne zu sehr sticht, unter einem Feigen- oder Johannisbrotbaum aneinandergeschmiegt eine bewegungslose Gruppe bilden. Manchmal sind die Zweige mit Stöcken abgestützt, ein sinnloser Versuch, den Schatten zu verlängern und der ganzen Herde unter diesem improvisierten Dach Raum zu geben.

Eines der heitersten und friedvollsten Dörfer Mallorcas, Valldemossa, liegt umgeben von Bergen auf einem stufenförmigen Abhang mit Stützmäuerchen (marges) in der Serra de Tramuntana. Ihre abschüssigen Straßen voller Balkone und Türen mit Blumentöpfen verwandeln den Ort in ein kleines Paradies. Die Schriftstellerin George Sand und ihr Geliebter, der Komponist Frédéric Chopin, verbrachten einen Winter in dem Kartäuserkloster von Valldemossa (1838–39). Im Prinzip wurde dieses Gebäude als königlicher Palast konzipiert, es wurde jedoch zu einem Kloster, als im Jahre 1399 Kartäusermönche einzogen. Ebenfalls einen Besuch wert sind der Palast des Königs Sanxo (Palau del Rei Sanxo) und die Kirche von Sant Bartomeu.

This panoramic view shows one of the most virgin settings in the center of Ibiza. It is the little village of Santa Agnès; around there lie a few, well-spaced out country houses.

Eine der noch unberührtesten Gegenden im Herzen Ibizas enthüllt dieser Blick auf das kleine Dorf von Santa Agnès mit den rundherum verstreuten rustikalen Häusern.

Sights to cheer up your soul: the splendor of the blossoming almond trees.

Eindrücke, die die Seele erfreuen: die Pracht der Mandelbäume in voller Blüte ...

The way to the Illetas beach (Formentera).

Many artists and sculptors who live on the Pitiusas Isles (Formentera and Ibiza) have tried to reflect the beauty of the savine in their works.

Savine (red cedar) is a highly valued wood used in the roofs, door frames and windows of old country cottages.

Der Weg zum Strand von Illetas (Formentera).

Zahlreiche Künstler und Bildhauer, die auf den Pitiusen leben, haben versucht, die Schönheit der Zedern in ihren Werken festzuhalten.

Das Holz der Zeder ist sehr geschätzt, und wir finden es in den Deckenbalken, an den Schwellen der Türen und den Fensterstürzen der alten Bauernhäuser.

On the way to the hamlet of Sant Mateu (Ibiza).

The working clothes of the Ibizian farmers have not changed much over the years, but scenes like this may soon fade away as few people now rely on working the land for their livelihood.

Work clothes are different to those worn on festive days when the natives dress themselves up in a skirt over which there goes an apron and an elaborate shawl (chal) to cover the body. A headscarf partially covers the long, lovingly pleated ponytail adorned with a bow. Sometimes even local folk wear a wide-rimmed straw hat to protect themselves from harsh sun-rays.

Dorfstraße in Sant Mateu (Ibiza).

Die Arbeitskleidung der Bauersfrauen von Ibiza hat sich im Verlauf der Jahre nur wenig verändert, aber auch dieses Bild wird mit der Zeit verloren gehen, denn es gibt nur noch wenige, die von der Arbeit auf dem Lande leben.

Die Arbeitskleidung unterscheidet sich deutlich vom Festkleid mit langem Rock und der Schürze darüber, dazu ein reich bestickter Schal, der den Körper umhüllt. Auf dem Kopf verdeckt ein Kopftuch einen Teil des langen, sorgfältig geflochtenen Zopfes, der mit einer Schleife geschmückt ist; manchmal tragen die Frauen einen breitkrempigen Strohhut, der sie vor den Sonnenstrahlen schützt.

A view of the surroundings of Santa Gertrudis (Ibiza).

Ein Blick auf die Umgebung von Santa Gertrudis (Ibiza).

These photos give an idea about some of the architectural characteristics of the islands. Country people tend to whitewash the walls of their homes applying a mixture of paint and water with a brush. However, if the walls are left their natural stone or sand color then the door and window frames, and other features like the door seen in the photo hiding away the pipes, are normally marked out with whitewash.

Auf diesen Fotos kann man einige Elemente der Inselarchitektur bewundern. Die Bauersfrauen weißen die Mauern der Häuser mit Hilfe eines Besens und einer Mischung aus Kalk und Wasser. Wenn die Wand jedoch in der natürlichen Farbe der Steine oder des zum Verputz verwendeten Sandes belassen wird, werden mit dieser Mischung Türen, Fenster und andere Elemente umrahmt, wie zum Beispiel hier auf dem Foto die Tür einer Zisterne.

A group of houses in Balafia (Ibiza).

The houses are laid out blending in with the lie of the land; they are lined up into rows on different levels defined by great stone slabs and small white-washed steps. The primitive simplicity and austerity stands out in an architecture that permits neither the superfluous nor the decorative.

In the background a circular tower holds its own. Its windows and doors are marked off with whitewash. These towers are very characteristics of the islands and form part of their heritage and history: they were both a means of defense and mills for grinding the wheat.

Detail einer Häusergruppe in Balafia (Ibiza).

Die Lage der Häuser passt sich an die Landschaft an; kleine Sträßchen, gepflastert mit großen Steinplatten, und niedrige, mit Kalk gestrichene Treppen geben ihnen ihre Ordnung. Ins Auge fällt die primitive Einfachheit und Strenge der Gruppe, in dessen Architektur Überflüssiges und Dekoration keinen Platz haben.

Im Hintergrund fällt ein Wehrturm mit runder Grundfläche auf, dessen Öffnungen ebenfalls mit ungelöschtem Kalk eingerahmt sind. Diese für die Inseln so charakteristischen Türme sind Teil ihres historischen und kulturellen Erbes: sie wurden als Verteidigungsgebäude oder als Mühlen für landwirtschaftliche Zwecke genutzt.

This is how a typical oven looked in the majority of homes in the country. The domed cover was standard.

The small windows which allow in light but keep out the heat in summer and the cold in winter are common in the homes of ordinary country-folk.

Hier sehen wir einen typischen ländlichen Ofen mit seiner kuppelförmigen Überdachung, wie er in den meisten Bauernhäusern zu finden ist.

Die kleinen Gitterfenster, die die Helligkeit durchlassen, aber Hitze und Kälte Einhalt gebieten, gehören zur ländlichen Architektur.

Saint Eulària church, Saint Rafel church, Saint Eulària church (again), Saint Gertrudis church (from left to right and from top to bottom).

The style of churches on Ibiza has been developed since the middle ages and slightly modified in modern times. They are known as fortified churches due to the external aspect somewhat reminiscent of a stronghold. However, this has not encroached on their refinement manifested through numerous nuances that render each one unique in its own way. One external element they all have in common is the espadanya containing the bell to call the faithful to prayer. Other shared features are the half-pointed arched portals and the small windows with lintels.

Kirche von Sta. Eulária, Kirche von Sant Rafale, Kirche von Sta. Eulária, Kirche von Sta. Gertrudis (von links nach rechts und von oben nach unten).

Auf Ibiza findet man ein Kirchenmodell, das auf das Mittelalter zurückgeht, seitdem weiterentwickelt und bis in die Moderne hinein immer wieder umgestaltet wurde; diese Gotteshäuser sind mit ihrem festungsartigen Aussehen als Wehrkirchen bekannt. Die Schönheit dieser Bauten spiegelt sich in zahlreichen Nuancen, die ihre Individualität ausmachen. Allen gemein ist die espadanya, der Glockenturm mit der Glocke, die die Gläubigen zum Gebet ruft. Weitere gemeinsame Elemente sind das gewölbte Bogenportal und die kleinen Fenster.

The Saint Francesc Xavier church (Ibiza) is alongside the road leading to Les Salines. If you continue along the road it will take you to the spectacular views over the salt plains and then on to the two largest sandy beaches on the island, Es Cavallet and Les Salines beach.

Die Kirche von Sant Francesc Xavier (Ibiza) liegt an der Strasse nach Les Salines. Wenn man den Weg weitergeht, hat man einen eindrucksvollen Blick auf die Salinen und im Hintergrund auf die beiden größten Sandstrände Ibizas, den Es Cavallet und den Strand von Les Salines.

Next page:
Sant Llorenç church (Ibiza)
A close up of the niche containing the three crosses, a motif found in other churches on the island such as the Saint Gertrudis church.

Folgende Seite:
Die Kirche von Sant Llorenç (Ibiza).
Ein Detail der bogenförmigen Nische mit drei Kreuzen. Dieses Motiv findet man auch in anderen Kirchen, zum Beispiel in der Kirche von Sta. Gertrudis.

Panoramic view of the interior of the isle of Menorca (upper photo).

Naveta de Es Tudons, Menorca (lower photo).

Menorca has an important archeological heritage, highly representative of the Balearic Islands as a whole.
In 1993 it was designated a World Cultural and Natural Heritage site by Unesco in recognition of the harmony between the social-economic development and the preservation of the natural environment and the artistic and cultural patrimony.

Panorama im Herzen der Insel Menorca (oben).

Ein megalithisches Monument in Form eines umgedrehten Schiffes (naveta) in Es Tudons (unten).

Innerhalb der Inselgruppe der Balearen verfügt Menorca über bedeutende archäologische Schätze.
Im Jahr 1993 erklärte die UNESCO sie in Anerkennung der Harmonie zwischen der sozio-ökonomischen Entwicklung, der Erhaltung der Umwelt sowie den künstlerisch-kulturellen Werten zum Weltkultur- und Naturerbe.

A megalithic monument on Menorca which is known as a taula. They are constructed out of enormous blocks of rough-hewed stone -les taules. These archeological sites are a significant part of the Minorcan landscape, attracting archeologists from all round the world, keen to investigate the surprising cultural heritage of the Balearic Islands.

Ein megalithisches Monument in Menorca mit dem Namen Taula (Tisch). Die Taulas, erbaut mit riesigen, grob behauenen Steinblöcken und die archäologischen Vorkommen sind ein wichtiger Bestandteil der menorquinischen Landschaft. Archäologen aus aller Welt besuchen und untersuchen diese überraschenden Schätze der Balearen.

La cartuja de Valldemossa, the monastery of Valldemossa, was originally constructed to be a royal palace. Events turned out differently and it ended up occupied by Carthusian monks in 1399.

Die Cartuja, das Kartäuserkloster in Valldemossa, wurde ursprünglich als königlicher Palast errichtet und im Jahre 1399 von den Mönchen in Besitz genommen.

Views of Montuiri (above); Llubi (above right); Aimari (center); and Buger (below).

Ansichten von Montuiri (oben), Llubi (rechts oben), Aimari (Mitte) und Buger (unten).

A far cry from the rugged, rocky precipices along the coast, the interior of the island is flat and therefore ideal for growing cereals.

Weit entfernt von den zerklüfteten Küsten des Nordens herrschen im Inselinneren weite Ebenen vor, die sich hervorragend für den Getreideanbau eignen.

Outdoor Living: in the Country
Draussen Leben: Auf dem Land

Outdoor Living: in the Country

On the road that goes from Palma to Sóller, at the foot of the Tramuntana mountain range, there are possessió houses which still preserve the designer's original artistic embellishments and the architectural features, as well as the layout of the gardens. Near to Bunyola there are the gardens of Alfàbia and Raixa, Sa Granja in Esporles and Son Marroig in Valldemossa.

Another calling point on any tour should be the market of Sineu in the main square of the vila of Fossar. It is the busiest livestock market on Mallorca and dates back to the fourteenth century when it was granted a royal privilege to trade in animals by Pere el Ceremoniós. The covered market hall standing today was reformed in 1956, but the original drinking trough from the sixteenth century has been conserved, though it was reformed in 1904, as has the Pou des Triquet, the well of Triquet, (1565). Every Wednesday the market is brought to life by the buzz of typical rural trading, intrinsically linked to the Mallorquin country way of life.

Another market which feels good to stroll around taking in its hippy air as you look at the clothes and glass and silver beads is the Las Dalias market between Santa Eulària and Sant Carles on Ibiza. Its open, relaxed and stimulating ambience has risen to the fame of the Es Canar, an older and more traditional market.

In the little villages life goes on at a graceful pace. In the afternoons the locals often stroll around the village square. In Sóller, for example, not only can you have a coffee or a beer while enjoying a relaxed chat, also you can contemplate the church of Sant Bartomeu which together with the Banc de Sóller building makes up an interesting set of modernist - also known as art nouveau - buildings.

Everyone in all the valley of Sóller enters into the spirit of the regional festival La Fira i el Firó, held to celebrate the victory over the Corsairs on May 11, 1561. The festivities consist of mock battles in which the locals dress up as corsairs and peasants. The clashes take place - there are four of them and the festivities go on for twelve hours - once the opening speech, el pregón, has been read in the village square. The participants advance with shotguns firing blanks and letting off bangers. However, they stop to eat and drink as they move around the circuit. The day's typical dish is snails with alioli, a sauce made from garlic and olive oil.

Draussen leben: auf dem Land

An der Straße von Palma nach Sóller, am Fuße der Serra de Tramuntana, liegen einige Landgüter (possessions), die sowohl im Hinblick auf die Architektur als auch auf die Anlage ihrer Gärten in ihrer ursprünglichen Gestaltung erhalten geblieben sind. In der Nähe von Bunyola sind das die Gärten von Alfàbia und Raix, Sa Granja in Esporles, Son Marroig in Valldemossa ...

Ein weiterer lohnender Besuch gilt dem Markt von Sineu auf dem zentralen Dorfplatz, genannt fossar. Es ist der am besten besuchte traditionelle Viehmarkt Mallorcas. Er geht auf das 14. Jahrhundert zurück als der alte fossar infolge eines königlichen Sonderrechts von Pedro III. (Pere el Ceremoniós) in einen Tiermarkt umgestaltet wurde. Die heutige überdachte Markthalle ist das Ergebnis eines Umbaus im Jahre 1956; die Tränke (abeurador) aus dem 16. Jahrhundert blieb jedoch erhalten und wurde 1904 renoviert, ebenso der Brunnen Pou des Triquet (1565). Jeden Mittwoch kann man das Treiben und die Farbenpracht einer Geschäftigkeit beobachten, die ihre Wurzeln im typischen Landhandel Mallorcas hat.

Noch ein reizvoller Markt, freundlich und mit stilechter Hippie-Atmosphäre, auf dem mit Kleidung und Silberwaren gehandelt wird, ist der Markt von Las Dalias zwischen Santa Eulària und Sant Carles auf Ibiza. Mit seinem offenen, lebhaften und kunterbunten Ambiente ist er inzwischen so bekannt wie ein anderer Markt mit ähnlicher Atmosphäre geworden, der jedoch älter und traditioneller ist: der Markt von Es Canar.

Das Leben auf den Dörfern spielt sich sehr ruhig ab; am Nachmittag verlassen die Menschen ihre Häuser und drehen eine Runde um den Platz. Sóller ist ein Beispiel hierfür: auf dem Hauptplatz kann man einen Kaffee oder ein Bier trinken und über das Wetter reden oder über sonst etwas Unwichtiges. Man kann aber auch die Kirche von Sant Bartomeu bewundern, die zusammen mit dem Gebäude der Bank von Sóller einen sehr interessanten Jugendstil-Komplex bildet.

Ein im ganzen Tal von Sóller verschwenderisch gefeiertes Fest ist La Fira i El Firó, das an den Sieg über die türkischen Korsaren am 11. Mai 1561 erinnert. Die Festakte lassen die Schlacht wieder aufleben, wozu sich die Einwohner als Piraten, Bauern und Bäuerinnen verkleiden. Die Konfrontation findet nach der Rede zur Eröffnung der Festlichkeiten auf dem Dorfplatz statt. Die Schlachten, es sind insgesamt vier, und das Fest dauern fast zwölf Stunden; die Teilnehmer rücken mit Flinten und Feuerwerkskörpern vor und werden dort, wo sie vorbeikommen, zum Essen und Trinken eingeladen. Das typische Gericht an diesem Tag sind Schnecken mit Knoblauchmayonnaise (alioli).

This delightful view shows how a design brief can fully respect traditional architecture, perfectly integrating it into a rural setting, making the most of both aspects and yet placing a premium on obtaining maximum comfort.

Ein wunderbares Beispiel für die perfekte Integration von moderner Gestaltung in der ländlichen Umgebung. Hier wird die traditionelle Architektur nicht nur respektiert, sondern hervorgehoben – verbunden mit einem Maximum an Behaglichkeit und Komfort.

These marvelously designed gardens set in heavenly surroundings enable us to be transported away in dreams to anywhere in the world. The objective is to create a relaxing environment in the heart of the Balearic countryside.

Diese liebevoll gestalteten Gärten und Innenhöfe sind Orte zum Träumen, die uns in Gedanken an jeden beliebigen Flecken der Erde bringen können. Die Kunst besteht darin, ein geeignetes Plätzchen zu finden – wie diese hier auf dem Land im Herzen der Balearen.

Creating delightful corners for enjoying a relaxing siesta, or for sitting under a shady porch to read an intriguing book, is easy with this climate imbued in tranquility.

Die Einrichtung gemütlicher Eckchen, um eine kuschelige Siesta zu halten oder um sich mit einem Buch in der Hand in den Schatten einer Veranda zu setzen, ist sehr einfach in diesem Klima, das selbst so deutlich Ruhe ausstrahlt.

IBIZA

20

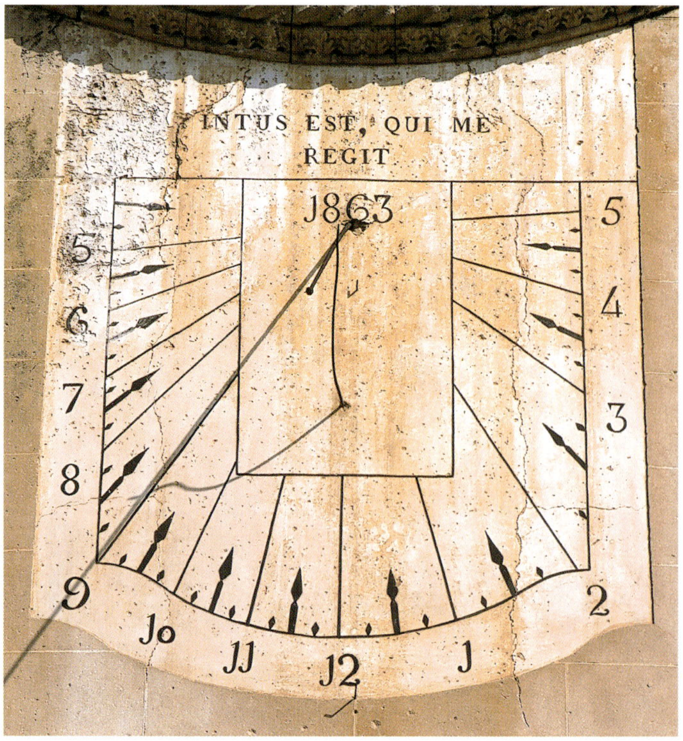
INTUS EST, QUI ME
REGIT
J863

EXTRA SWEET

Different pictures of the markets of Pobla and Sineu (Mallorca)
The local markets bring color to the squares where they are held and are the ideal time and place for shopping, chatting with the neighbors or just relaxing over a coffee.

Verschiedene Eindrücke der Märkte von Sa Pobla und Sineu (Mallorca). Die Märkte in den Dörfern verleihen den öffentlichen Plätzen, auf denen sie stattfinden, Farbe und Leben und sind der ideale Ort, um einzukaufen, mit den Nachbarn ein Schwätzchen (la xerradeta) zu halten und einen Kaffee zu trinken.

aPrevious page: The tourists are impressed by the remarkable variety of products on offer in the markets: fruit, vegetables and even traditional Mallorcan honey liquor.

Auf der vorherigen Seite: Das vielfältige Angebot der Märkte zieht ganz besonders die Aufmerksamkeit der Besucher an: Obst und Gemüse – sowohl frisch als auch getrocknet – und der traditionelle mallorquinische Honiglikör.

Te Limon
Lavanda
Salvia
Te Manzana
Flor Azahar
Estigma Maiz
Boldo
Diabetes
Te Naranja
Cola Caballo
Eucalipto
Sen Hoja
Colesterol
Reuma
Varices
Te Negro Ceylan
Sen Foliculos
Hierba Luisa
Regaliz Natural
Valeriana
Guarana
Menta
Te verde

Handicrafts are another part of the Mediterranean cultural heritage which have stood up to the trends of modern society and manufacturing processes. The archduke Luis Salvador kept a detailed record of all the ways of manufacturing baskets on the islands.

In the photo on the right you can see elaborate embroidery work by Joana Villalonga (Mallorca).

Das Kunsthandwerk ist einer der Werte der mediterranen Kultur, die sich in der Gesellschaft von heute gehalten haben. Der Erzherzog Luis Salvador machte eine detaillierte Inventur der verschiedenen Herstellungsarten von Korbwaren auf den Inseln.

Auf dem Foto rechts ist eine reiche Stickerei von Joana Villalonga (Mallorca) zu sehen.

Glass blowing came to Mallorca from the east, influenced by the Moorish and Venetian traditions. Today artisanal kilns can still be found manufacturing glass decorations for table-tops, lighting and other sundry ornaments. Oven at Menestralia glaziery (above); typical glassware and ceramic sign of the Gordiola glass factory (left); both located in Mallorca.

Die Glasbläserei kam mit Einflüssen der Araber und Venedigs aus dem Orient nach Mallorca. Heute sind noch einige der Glashütten in Betrieb und stellen schöne Objekte für die Tafel, in Form von Leuchtern oder für die verschiedensten Zwecke her, die oft als Dekorationselemente Verwendung finden. Glasofen von Menestralia (oben), Produkte und das Keramikschild von Gordiola (links); beide Glashütten sind auf Mallorca.

Clay has always been the raw material traditionally used for making kitchen pots. Dishes for storing cheese, salt pots, sugar bowls, casseroles used for flipping omlettes and salad bowls are all necessary. A typical finish: glazed ceramic with a yellow trim and, very importantly, the name of the food to be stored in it.

Ton ist das Material, aus dem seit Generationen die Küchenutensilien hergestellt werden: Schalen und Schüsseln zur Aufbewahrung von Käse, Salz, Zucker, um die Tortilla, das spanische Omelett, zu wenden, für Salat und tausend weitere Möglichkeiten. Ein typisches Dekor: glasierter gebrannter Ton mit schlichten gelben Mustern und – das ist wichtig – dem Namen des Nahrungsmittels, für das es gedacht ist.

Fire, processions, parades with the locals turned out in traditional dress, and strutting horses (in Menorca) are the main spectacles any visitor lucky enough to be on the islands during the fiestas can admire.

Feuer, Prozessionen, Trachtenumzüge und Vorführungen mit Pferden (auf Menorca) sind die wichtigsten Veranstaltungen, die der Besucher miterleben kann, der das Glück hat, einem der Feste auf der Insel beizuwohnen.

Lorenzina, on the road that joins Ibiza to Santa Eulàlia, is a recently opened, groundbreaking shop. The owners, passionately in love with Mediterranean culture, bought the products on display in their shop on their travels in Morroco, Italy, Spain, France and Turkey, as if they were for decorating their own home. They sell everything from textile garments and ironware through to cosmetics, perfumes and paint.

Lorenzina, an der Straße von Ibiza nach Santa Eulàlia gelegen, ist ein erst vor kurzem eröffnetes Geschäft mit einem innovativen Angebot. Die von der mediterranen Kultur begeisterten Eigentümer kaufen auf ihren Reisen durch Marokko, Italien, Spanien, Frankreich und die Türkei die verschiedensten Objekte, als ob sie ihr eigenes Haus einrichten wollten. Das Sortiment besteht aus Textilien, kleinen dekorativen Gegenständen aus Eisen, Parfums, Bildern ...

Coconut Company, in Manacor, sells a wide range of high quality furniture for the home. The company designs its own pieces in wood, but also sells other designers' products and decorations, all of them exhibited in these spacious premises.

Coconut Company in Manacor (Mallorca) offeriert eine breitgefächerte Auswahl qualitativ hochwertiger Einrichtungsgegenstände. Möbel aus Holz, die von der Firma selbst entworfen werden, Haushaltsutensilien oder Deko-Objekte sind nur einige der Vorschläge, die dem Besucher in diesem weitläufigen Ladenlokal unterbreitet werden.

Hotel Les Terrasses

The Balearics have plenty to brag about on the hotel front and this delightfully cozy one is on Ibiza, alongside the one kilometer road marker as you drive out of the city towards Santa Eulàlia des Riu. Part of its charm stems from it being off the beaten track and thus difficult to find. However, if you are blessed enough to get there you are sure to find all the pleasures of vacationing Ibiza style. When coming along the main road, look out for the blue-painted stone, the only reference point, four kilometers before Santa Eulàlia where you turn off onto a track. The hotel is at the end.

The hotel consists of a traditionally Ibizian country house with eight guest rooms in bungalows. They are surrounded by gardens gently falling away in terraces towards the main house. The way the whole space has been conceived and the exquisite, personal decoration are the work of the owner, Françoise Tialoux.

Among the green and beautifully manicured gardens, there lie two swimming pools. All the details are aimed at making the guests in this renovated old farmhouse feel really at home. In the main building there is a kitchen where all the food is cooked, a dining room and spaces for relaxing or simply reading or passing the time with the family. The prepared cuisine can be leisurely eaten in the open air on the wide terracing.

The stone façades of the lodgings blend in harmoniously with the style of the whole project. Each bedroom has its own style of decoration that creates a very personal atmosphere, from the most modern feel through to an air of romance.

Dieses charmante und behagliche Hotel liegt auf der Insel Ibiza, am Km.1 der Landstraße von der Inselhauptstadt nach Sta. Eulàlia des Riu. Einen Teil seines Reizes macht schon allein die Schwierigkeit aus, es überhaupt zu finden. Es liegt ganz in der Absicht der Hoteliers, dass nur ein paar Auserwählte hierher gelangen, die auf der Suche nach einem Urlaub im reinsten Stil dieses Insel-Paradieses sind. Ungefähr vier Kilometer vor Sta. Eulàlia stößt man auf einen Weg, der als einziger deutlicher Hinweis mit einem blau gestrichenen Stein markiert ist. Diesem Weg muss man bis zum Ende folgen.

Das Hotel ist ein Landhaus im traditionellen ibizenkischen Stil mit acht Zimmern in Bungalows, die vom Haupthaus abgetrennt und weitläufig von Gärten umgeben sind; diese Gärten führen über Terrassen bis zum Haupthaus herab. Die Konzeption der Anlage und die exklusive wie persönliche Dekoration ist ein Werk der Eigentümerin Françoise Tialoux.

Zwischen den grünen und liebevoll gepflegten Gärten liegen zwei fantastische Swimming Pools. In diesem alten Bauernhaus wird wirklich alles unternommen, damit der Gast sich "wie zu Hause" fühlt. Im Haupthaus befinden sich die Gemeinschaftsräume: Küche, Salon, Speisesaal und gemütliche Räume zum Lesen und Entspannen in einer heimeligen und sehr familiären Atmosphäre. Gäste und Freunde des Hauses können die Köstlichkeiten aus der Küche im Freien auf einer der großzügigen Terrassen genießen.

Die Zimmer fügen sich perfekt in das Ensemble mit seinen klassischen steinernen Fassaden ein. Jedes einzelne Zimmer ist in einem anderen Stil dekoriert und jedes hat seine persönliche Note: von romantisch bis modern.

Upon entering the hotel you will notice singularities typical of a country house, such as the old cistern, the thick white-washed walls and the indigo blue-painted window frames which conjure up a placid, bright and upbeat atmosphere. This is how to slow time down and to get away from the summer hustle and bustle of the city of Eivissa, just a few kilometers away.

Der Eingang zum Hotel weist die typischen Details eines Landhauses auf: eine alte Zisterne, dicke, weiß gestrichene Mauern und Indigoblau umrahmte Fenster, die eine angenehme Atmosphäre schaffen, leuchtend und heiter zugleich. Es ist ein idealer Ort, um dem Tohuwabohu der Inselhauptstadt zu entfliehen, mitten in der Hochsaison und nur einen Katzensprung entfernt.

162
16.204

These marvelous little corners nestling among the vegetation typical of the islands, such as the bougainvillaea found in so many country house gardens, are ideal retreats for finding peace and tranquil idleness.

Typisch für die Vegetation der Inseln ist die Bougainvillea, die in den Gärten vieler Landhäuser wächst. Sie schmückt diese wunderbaren Ecken, die ideale Rückzugsorte sind, um zur Ruhe zu kommen und genüsslich zu entspannen.

Swimming pools set in a paradise, with comfortable hammocks strewn around them, fit the bill when you do not feel like going down to the beach, despite the hotel's proximity to stunning coves and divine inlets.

Die Swimming Pools in paradiesischer Umgebung und mit gemütlichen Liegen sind wie geschaffen für die Tage, an denen man nicht an den Strand gehen will, obwohl es nicht weit vom Hotel einige der schönsten Buchten und Strände gibt.

The way the bedrooms have been decorated gives an idea of the depth of the owner's personal involvement. Each room has its own unique style.

In the kitchen everything has been thought out to satisfy the guests with a rich collection of memorable Mediterranean tastes and textures.

Die Details der Dekoration geben einen guten Eindruck von dem persönlichen Geschmack, mit dem die Zimmer von der Eigentümerin eingerichtet wurden – jedes in einem anderen Stil.

In der Küche steht alles bereit, um den Appetit der Gäste mit den leckersten Gerichten der mediterranen Küche zu stillen.

Hotel Son Gener

This old possessió dwelling on the road from Manacor to Artà, on Mallorca, is a fine example of how country houses used to be constructed on the island. The building dates from the eighteenth century when it was used for olive oil production. The old tafona has been preserved. Near it you can see a talayot, one of the prehistoric stone towers found in the Balearic Islands.

The hotel's unsurpassable backdrop is the Serra de Llevant. Close at hand there are splendid, ruggedly beautiful coves and the village of Artà.

The hotel, subtly merging into the lie of the land, comes as a pleasant surprise to peace and countryside lovers. In its grounds there is a water deposit for irrigating the garden and an enormous swimming pool for cooling off when the sun burns brightest.

Inside the possessió the ambience is fresh and invigorating. The thick walls keep the warmth in during winter, and mitigate the sultriness in summer. There are plenty of porches and semi-open spaces which put you in the frame of mind for resting.

Dieses alte Landgut wurde als Hotel umgebaut; es liegt an der Landstraße von Manacor nach Artà auf der Insel Mallorca und ist ein anschauliches Beispiel für den Baustil der mallorquinischen Landhäuser. In dieser Finca aus dem 18. Jahrhundert wurde früher Öl hergestellt, die alte Ölpresse, tafona, ist noch erhalten. Außerdem befindet sich in seiner unmittelbaren Nähe auch ein prähistorischer steinerner Turm, ein talayot.

Zur unvergleichlichen Umgebung des Hotels gehört die Serra de Llevant, die sich im Hintergrund erhebt. Nicht weit entfernt gibt es außerdem traumhafte Buchten mit einzigartigen Naturschönheiten und ein typisch ländliches Dorf, Artà.

Das hervorragend in die Landschaft integrierte Hotel ist eine angenehme Überraschung für alle Liebhaber des Landlebens und der Ruhe. Auf dem Grundstück befindet sich ein großer Wasserspeicher zur Bewässerung und ein geräumiger Pool, um sich in den heißesten Stunden des Tages aufs Angenehmste zu erfrischen.

Das Innere des Landguts strahlt eine frische und wohltuende Atmosphäre aus. Die dicken Steinmauern bewahren die Wärme im Winter und schützen vor ihr im Sommer. Viele Veranden und halb-offene Räume entführen die Gäste in ein entspanntes und friedliches Ambiente.

The façade of a typical Majorcan possessió of which the varied pattern in the stone and the arched portal, framed by voussoirs, commandeer your attention.

Die Fassade eines klassischen mallorquiner Landgutes. Die Bauweise aus unbehauenen Steinen und das typische Eingangsportal mit einem Rundbogen, der von Keilsteinen aus dem einheimischen Kalkstein Marès eingerahmt ist, fallen ins Auge.

In the upper photo you can see how big the water deposit is, and in the background the Llevant mountain range. The simplicity of these country houses mean that there are no hassles, no worries, just everything you need for a restful stay.

Auf dem oberen Foto erkennt man die beeindruckende Größe des Wasserreservoirs; den Hintergrund bildet die Serra de Llevant. Die Schlichtheit dieser alten Landhäuser vermittelt Stille und Gelassenheit, es bleibt kein Platz für Hektik und Stress.

The old tafona, a mill for olive oil, stands out amidst the traditional architecture and the photo shows how it has been used in the hothouse area for different plants.

In dieser märchenhaften Kulisse traditioneller Inselarchitektur fällt die alte Ölpresse im Hintergrund auf. Wie in einem Pflanzkübel gedeihen in ihr die verschiedensten Pflanzen und Blumen.

Secluded Artist's Studio

This original architectural project situated in the heart of the countryside in the center of Ibiza is the studio-cum-home of the painter Miguel Buades. The original design brief, the work of the artist himself, stipulated that the external structure had to be similar to a warehouse or depot.

The rectangular, flat-roofed building has two entrances and is practically lacking in windows. The main entrance, very wide and north-facing, leads into the studio. The other entrance, on one side of the building, is a sliding door accessing into the residential quarters. Intense light comes in through four skylights equipped with an inventive device enabling them to be adjusted. This is one of the key components of the plan as playing with their position gives rise to distinct effects and ambiences.

The interior is one space for the studio, living room and bedroom. This area is separated off from the kitchen and bathroom, at the far end, by a divider on which one of the artist's pieces is displayed.

A terrific breakfast in the midst of the forest, under some shady trees, will stand the painter in good creative stead, giving him the necessary tranquility with which to start the day.

Künstlerhaus in der Abgeschiedenheit

Dieses originelle Haus, mitten auf dem Land im Herzen der Insel Ibiza gelegen, ist das Wohn-Studio des Malers Miguel Buades. Eine Grundidee für den Entwurf, der vom Künstler selbst gestaltet wurde, war, dass die äußere Struktur einer Halle oder einem Lagerschuppen ähneln sollte.

Das Gebäude mit eckigem Grundriss und Flachdach hat zwei Eingänge und praktisch keine Fenster. Der Haupteingang ist sehr breit und liegt nach Norden hin, von hier gelangt man direkt ins Atelier; der andere befindet sich in der seitlichen Fassade, wo eine Schiebetür in den Wohnbereich führt. Licht fällt reichlich durch die vier flachen Oberlichter ein und kann durch eine originelle im Dach eingebaute Vorrichtung reguliert werden. Diese Elemente sind der Schlüssel zur Architektur dieses Hauses, da man je nach Positionierung mit der Helligkeit spielen kann.

Der Innenraum ist ein nicht untergliederter großer Raum, in dem sich das Atelier und ein Wohn-Schlafzimmer befinden. Eine einzige Wand mit einem Werk des Künstlers trennt diesen Bereich von der Küche und dem Bad ab.

Ein herrliches Frühstück mitten im Wald, im Schatten der Bäume, inspiriert den Maler oder gibt ihm die nötige Ruhe, den Tag zu beginnen.

The ingenious light regulator situated above the skylight forms an original exterior structure; multiplied by four they give a distinct visual rhythm to the roof.

A view of the entrance into the studio-cum-home showing an outdoor table protected by a sunshade, under which the soirées can go on in intimate contact with the natural surroundings.

Die ausgetüftelten Oberlichter verleihen mit ihrer originellen Form und ihrer Positionierung auf dem Dach der Fassade je nach Blickwinkel einen eigenen Rhythmus.

Ansicht eines der Eingänge zum Atelier-Haus. Ein langer Tisch mit einem Sonnenschirm wurde aufgestellt, damit man die Tage im direkten Kontakt mit der umgebenden Natur ausklingen lassen kann.

Some small details and the way they are set out emphasize the human side of this ordered space, and tell us something about everyday life here. The piled logs for firewood are for keeping warm in winter, clothes can be hung out to dry between the pine trees, and the stone drinking trough is a vestige from the times when animals were kept.

Einige Details verraten die menschlichen Eingriffe in der Anordnung und Verteilung bestimmter Gegenstände, die uns vom Alltag berichten: Der Holzstapel, um sich im Winter zu wärmen, die zwischen den Pinien zum Trocknen aufgehängte Wäsche, der steinerne Wassertrog …

The painter's studio-cum-house. In the foreground we can see his worktable with all his equipment laid out. (upper photo)
The living quarters, except for the kitchen and bathroom, are in no way separated from the studio. One of the artist's oeuvres hangs on a wall-like divider, not quite touching the ceiling, to mark off these two spaces. (lower photo)

Gesamtansicht des Wohn-Studios. Im Vordergrund ist der Arbeitstisch des Malers mit seinen Werkzeugen zu sehen (oben).
Der als Wohnraum vorgesehene Bereich hat keinerlei Trennwände zum Atelier, einzig Bad und Küche sind hinter einer Wand verborgen, die mit einem der Kunstwerke des Malers dekoriert ist.

The most intimate things about a person are revealed by their bedroom and their creative work.

Einblick in die Persönlichkeit einer Person gewährt die Privatsphäre ihrer Wohnung sowie ihre kreative Arbeit ...

A House in the Country

This house is in the middle of the Mallorcan countryside near to the village of Sant Llorenç. It was an old country house madeover and rendered habitable again but without extinguishing the innate qualities of the original structure.

Thomas Wegner, who designed and realized the project, started out working from the original structure which had included stores for produce and quarters for the livestock. The project took advantage of all this, of the way the rooms come off a central passageway, and of the lean-to roof to come up with a rustic home drawing on the beauty of the Mallorcan countryside around it.

The house is basically on the ground floor except that one of the two bedrooms has been created by using some of the space above the living area, thus bringing down the height of the ceiling. The marges (dry stone walls) and the tanca (wooden fence) have been conserved.

Three construction elements define the interior. The ceiling gives warmth to the atmosphere thanks to the commonly employed wooden beam structure. The windows in the solid walls have large panes framed by fine metal laminates ensuring more than adequate lighting inside. Finally the flooring is concrete in the bedrooms and living room but polished little stones are used in other areas such as the kitchen to give a genuinely rustic feel to the house as a whole.

In the dining area the contrast between the provincial atmosphere created by the large wooden table and benches in the middle and the "cutting edge" design of the lighting stands out.

Rustikale Villa

Dieses Landhaus in der Nähe des Dorfes Sant Llorenç auf Mallorca ist ein altes Gebäude, das unter Berücksichtigung der Gestaltungsregeln für die klassischen Landhäuser als Wohnhaus restauriert wurde. Die Grundstruktur des Gebäudes wurde früher als Lager für Landwirtschaftserzeugnisse und Stall benutzt. Thomas Wegner entwarf und realisierte dieses Modellprojekt, das einen weitläufigen Korridor und das schräge Pultdach nutzte, um ein rustikales Wohnhaus mitten in der mallorquinischen Landschaft zu schaffen.

Die Wohnräume befinden sich im Erdgeschoss mit Ausnahme eines Schlafzimmers, das in einer Dachstube eingerichtet wurde, die in einem Teil des Wohnraumes die Deckenhöhe verringert. Die alten Mauern aus trocken aufgeschichteten Steinen und der Holzzaun wurden beibehalten.

Drei Konstruktionselemente definieren den Innenraum: Die Decken schaffen dank der herkömmlichen Holzbalken eine warme Atmosphäre, während man die Fensteröffnungen in den dicken Mauern an das moderne System großer Glasscheiben mit feinen Metallrahmen angepasst hat, die reichlich Licht in den Innenraum hereinlassen. Der Fußboden in den Zimmern und im Wohnzimmer ist aus Presszement; er wird jedoch in einigen Bereichen des Hauses, wie zum Beispiel in der Küche, von eingelegten Kieseln unterbrochen, die dem Ganzen eine besonders rustikale Note geben.

In der Küche fällt der Gegensatz zwischen dem bäuerlichen Ambiente mit dem großen Tisch und den Holzbänken in der Mitte und den sehr originellen Designer-Lampen ins Auge.

The shade provided by the dense branches of the centenarian pine trees is a good place to enjoy relaxing open air meals.

Im Schatten der dichten Zweige der jahrhundertealten Pinien stellt der Garten des Hauses einen schönen Rahmen dar, um gemütlich im Freien zu essen.

It is evident and praiseworthy that the traditional architectural project aimed at perfectly integrating the house into the surroundings while inside a spacious, austere design has been created.

The decoration for this large, simple bedroom is nature itself framed by the glass door, not an artistic reproduction.

Stone and wood are the elements used to convey the rusticness in the design of this country home.

The iron-framed, glass doors tend to go unnoticed in the light of what can be seen outside beyond.

Der offensichtliche und löbliche Respekt vor der Umgebung zeigt sich hier in der Erhaltung der traditionellen Architektur, die perfekt an die Landschaft angepasst ist und gleichzeitig weitläufige und schlichte Räumlichkeiten im Inneren schafft.

Der Schmuck im großzügigen und einfachen Schlafzimmer ist das Bild hinter der verglasten Tür: die Natur selbst.

Stein und Holz sind die Elemente, aus denen sich diese rustikale Einrichtung, typisch für ein echtes Landhaus, zusammensetzt.

Die verglasten Türen mit eisernen Profilen scheinen sich angesichts des Blickes nach draußen aufzulösen.

Restored tradition

Rural buildings on Ibiza, simple and cheerful thanks to their immaculate whiteness, stick to the rules of traditional Mediterranean architecture so as to melt into the countryside. Built to suit the needs of the dwellers, yet stylish at the same time, they have a clean, fresh air to them. Starting out from the most minimum expression, a cube shape, features have been added on as new needs and ways of dealing with them arose.

This house was reformed with the aim of making living in it harmonious with nature. It takes full advantage of the outside as several elements of rustic furniture have been placed under the shelter of the natural cane porch, decorated by plants. The unpretentiousness of the furniture gives an intimate, personal air to the home, imbued in a profound tranquility. Everything adds up to make it the ideal refuge in which to hide away when the sun is most merciless.

The squat whitewashed walls, the intermittent small windows, the natural stone flooring and, at the back, the country oven, all make for a harmonious picture.

Bewahrte Tradition

Die rustikale, für Ibiza typische Konstruktion, einfach und fröhlich in ihrem makellosen Weiß, bleibt dem Vorbild der alten traditionellen Architektur des Mittelmeeres treu und bewahrt die perfekte Harmonie mit seiner ländlichen Umgebung. Maßgeschneidert für den Menschen gelingt die Schaffung eines reinen und frischen Ambientes, wo die Räumlichkeiten, die je nach Bedarf angebaut wurden, auf ein Minimum an Ausdruck, den Würfel, reduziert werden.

Dieses für ein Leben in Harmonie mit der Natur wieder wohnlich gemachte Haus nutzt den Innenraum und weitet ihn nach draußen aus, wo rustikale Möbel unter einem sympathischen strohbedeckten Vordach mit Pflanzendekoration stehen. Die Einfachheit des Mobiliars schafft eine intime und sehr persönliche Atmosphäre in einer Wohnung voller Frieden, die ein perfekter Zufluchtsort ist, wenn man während der heißesten Stunden vor der Sonne Schutz sucht.

Dicke, von kleinen Fenstern unterbrochene weiß getünchte Mauern, der Fußboden aus Naturstein und im Hintergrund der Bauernofen sind die Elemente dieses harmonischen Ensembles.

The outside of the house is an extension of inside. The pleasant shade is an ideal place for eating, just having a siesta or conversing with friends once the meal is over.

Der Außenraum ist als eine Erweiterung des Hauses gedacht, wo man im angenehmen Schatten seine Mahlzeiten einnimmt und danach die Siesta genießt oder unterhaltsame Tischgespräche führen kann.

Next pages:
Some doors and windows still have the original savine (red cedar) wood lintel.

The wooden beams of the ceiling, sometimes whitewashed, give new ambiental possibilities and in this case have permitted the creation of this lovely, cozy bedroom.

Little ideas make for a highly effective decoration. Here clay vases, recycled boards and a few plants embellish the home.

Auf den folgenden Seiten:
Bei einigen Türen und Fenstern ist noch der originale Sturz aus Zedernholz erhalten.

Die Decke aus gelegentlich auch getünchten Holzbalken wirkt leicht und verspielt und verleiht diesem romantischen und gemütlichen Schlafzimmer den Eindruck von Weite.

Kleine Dekorationsdetails, verschiedenartige Tonkrüge, alte Bohlen und üppige Pflanzen sind die Bestandteile der Dekoration dieses Hauses.

Simple Forms

This house, designed by Sergi Bastidas, B&B Estudio de Arquitectura, and situated near the town of Artà on Mallorca, is surrounded by an exceptional landscape the backdrop to which is the Llevant mountain range. One's attention is drawn to the simple lines and the open, luminous spaces that contrast with the construction elements, also used as purely decorative objects. The main façade, totally symmetrical, follows the dictates of traditional Mallorquin architecture. The entrance doorway uses truncated stone wedges to form a voussoir arch, a style also used to frame the small windows typical of the islands.

The corridor acts as an axis and leads into a bright, ample space where the dining room, living room and finally kitchen are located. The wooden beams, employed in the traditional manner throughout all the residence, are creative, as well as functional in the dining room, showing that it need not be a space just about eating. The effect is reinforced by the light, design orientated furniture. The upper floor, supported by two enormous round columns, is reached by a minimalist staircase, though the handrail has not been eliminated. The equilibrium in the design of the home is rounded off by the modern, down to earth yet functional furniture installed.

One enters the interior of this upbeat home walking over a pavement of rounded stones. The walls are grand windows which ensure the luminosity of the corridor in a deliberate effort to blur the dividing line between the house and the surrounding nature.

Reine Formen

Das von Sergi Bastidas, B&B Estudio de Arquitectura, entworfene Haus auf Mallorca liegt in der Nähe des Ortes Artá und bietet mit der Serra de Llevant im Hintergrund eine rundum außergewöhnliche Aussicht. Auffallend sind die einfachen Linien, die offenen und durchscheinenden Räume im Kontrast zu den baulichen Elementen, die als rein dekorative Objekte behandelt wurden. Die Hauptfassade ist vollkommen symmetrisch und hält sich an die Regeln der traditionellen mallorquinischen Architektur. Das Eingangstor besteht aus einem Bogen aus Keilsteinen (aus dem Kalkstein marés), die auch die kleinen, für diese Architektur typischen, Fenster umrahmen.

Der Gang markiert eine klare richtungsweisende Achse, die zu einem großzügigen und lichterfüllten Raum führt, der sich in Esszimmer, Wohnzimmer und Küche aufteilt. Das Holz der in allen Räumen traditionsgemäß angeordneten Balken erhält ein kreatives Moment in der Neuerstellung des Gebälks über dem Esszimmer, das mit zarten Designer-Möbeln eingerichtet ist. Der Zugang zur oberen Etage, die von zwei riesigen zylindrischen Pfeilern gestützt wird, geht über eine Freitreppe mit einem filigranen Geländer. Das Design der Wohnung wird durch modernes, jedoch funktionelles Mobiliar vervollständigt.

Der Zugang zu dieser hellen Wohnung führt über ein Pflaster aus runden Steinen. Ein lichterfüllter gläserner Gang ersetzt das Mauerwerk und stellt einen erfolgreichen Versuch dar, die Trennung zwischen Haus und Natur zu verwischen.

The main entrance typifies this unique home which combines all the traditional elements on the façade with modern and classical recourses inside.

Der Haupteingang verbindet alle Elemente dieses einmaligen Hauses, in dem sich das Zusammenspiel der traditionellen Elemente an der Außenfassade und der klassischen und modernen Lösungen im Innenraum vereint.

This double-height space lies beneath a wooden ceiling. Its spaciousness and the quality of light bring to mind a nave.

Unter einem Holzgebälk öffnet sich dieser weite und lichte Raum zu doppelter Höhe und erinnert an ein Schiffsdeck.

Next to the dining room a cozy living room with its own chimney emphasizes the togetherness of all the home: open and bathed in light. Two benches are covered by colorful cushions.

An das Esszimmer schließt sich ein gemütlicher Wohnraum mit offenem Kamin und zwei gemauerten Bänken mit fröhlichen Sitzkissen an. Großzügig und lichtdurchflutet, verbinden sich beide Bereiche zu einer wohnlichen Einheit.

On the upper floor there is a large room fitted out with comfortable couches as sweeping countryside and long stretches of sky are best viewed behind a large expanse of glass. The decoration details and ornaments have been kept to the minimum as the architectural style on its own is more than enough to give the room an adequate feel. On the ground floor, in one of the en-suite bathrooms, natural stone has been used instead of tiles.

Various details remind us just how powerfully expressive combining different materials – metal, wood and stone – can be in the design of a house.

Im oberen Teil befindet sich ein großer Raum mit komfortablen Diwanen, von denen aus man einen fantastischen Ausblick genießen kann. Die dekorativen Details wurden minimal gehalten, da der Raum durch sein eigenes architektonisches Design jeden Schmuck überflüssig macht. In der unteren Etage befinden sich zwei Zimmer und ein Bad, dessen Kacheln durch Naturstein ersetzt wurden.

Verschiedene Details vermitteln uns die ausdrucksvolle Kraft, die von der Kombination verschiedener Elemente wie Metall, Holz und Stein ausgeht.

White elegance

This home designed by Stéphane Bourgeois is in the Ibizian countryside. Its unpretentious external lines and the complete absence of superfluous adornments contrast with the sophistication inside.

On the ground floor the spaces are divided off by wide doors with lintels which combined with the continuous polished cement flooring give the sensation of spaciousness to the individual rooms. The ingenious design of the polished cement chimney at the back of the living room is highly visually impacting. In front of it there are two distinct, comfortable ambiences that ease you into a relaxed frame of mind, ideal for resting and unwinding.

Two features of the master bedroom come to the forefront: the inspired design of the bed and the bathtub standing on the floor breaking with all preconceived concepts about where baths should be. There is a shower in the bathroom surrounded by a floor of pebbles, a material traditionally used to prevent slipping outside the house and especially typical in the patios of country houses. The other bedroom combines sleeping and bathing in the same space but defines the zones by means of changes in the levels. The washbasin design is halfway between a classic sink and the very prevalent stone kitchen sinks.

The interior architectural design takes on the role of the furniture in an atmosphere where everything is kept simple and all the details are ironed out.

Weisse Eleganz

Dieses Haus auf Ibiza liegt auf dem Land und wurde von Stéphane Bourgeois entworfen. Die einfachen Linien der Außenansicht ohne Anspruch auf Ornamentik stehen im Gegensatz zu seinen ausgeklügelten Innenräumen.

Im Erdgeschoss werden die Räume durch breite, eckige Durchbrüche getrennt, die zusammen mit dem durchgehenden Fußboden aus poliertem Zement in den verschiedenen Bereichen den Eindruck von Weite vermitteln. Der Kamin im Hintergrund des Wohnzimmers, ebenfalls aus Zement, überrascht das Auge mit seinem exklusiven Design. Gegenüber befinden sich zwei komfortable Sitzecken zur verdienten Entspannung.

Das Hauptschlafzimmer spielt mit zwei auffallenden Elementen: einem Bett aus Mauerwerk und einer Badewanne direkt auf dem Fußboden im gleichen Zimmer. Im Badezimmer gibt es eine Dusche, die von einem Fußboden aus Kieselsteinen gerahmt wird, ein Material, das traditionsgemäß als rutschfester Belag in Außenbereichen verwendet wurde, zum Beispiel in den Höfen der Landhäuser. Auch im anderen Schlafzimmer befinden sich Bett und Badewanne im selben Raum. Die Bereiche sind hier jedoch durch unterschiedliche Ebenen voneinander getrennt. Das Design des Waschbeckens ist eine Mischung aus den antiken Waschbecken und den typischen Küchenspülbecken aus Stein.

Das architektonische Design der Innenräume ersetzt das Mobiliar in einer Umgebung, in der alles aus Mauerwerk geschaffen wurde.

The attractive interior design of the living room goes down well with the light tones and the natural light in a room where the clarity emphasizes the neatness of the decorative scheme.

There are so many spaces where this home exerts its therapy on you: behind every door you can find something different and therefore choose the most appropriate mood for each moment.

The chimney never fails to attract admiring looks and is the central axis of this design by Burgeois. A sliding door allows the living room and the house's relaxation zone to be isolated away from the rest of the areas.

Das attraktive Innendesign des Wohnzimmers passt gut zu den hellen Tönen und dem natürlichen Licht in einem Raum, in dem die Helligkeit und Stilreinheit der dekorativen Ausstattung den Ton angeben.

Die für Entspannung geschaffenen Räume sind zahlreich in diesem Haus, das sich hinter jedem Bogen verwandelt und in dem man sich je nach Stimmung immer einen idealen Platz aussuchen kann.

Der Kamin fungiert als ein visueller Magnet und bildet den zentralen Kern des Designs von Bourgeois. Durch eine Schiebetür können Wohnzimmer und Ruhezimmer vom Rest des Hauses getrennt werden.

The flooring run in all the home continues on into the large, bright kitchen.

Die weitläufige und helle Küche hat den gleichen Fußboden wie die restliche Wohnung.

The bedrooms, all of them brightly lit, are so originally designed that hardly any furnishings are necessary.

The white four-poster bed with its canopy harks back to old, classic bedrooms. The daring bathroom design mixes wooden flooring with rounded stones that prevent slipping.

Das Design der lichtdurchfluteten Zimmer verzichtet fast gänzlich auf Mobiliar.

Das Bett imitiert die barocken Schlafzimmer mit Baldachin und vier großen weißen Säulen als Rahmen, während das Bad von einem gewagten Design inspiriert wurde, in dem sich der Holzfußboden mit einem Boden aus rutschfesten Kieselsteinen abwechselt.

Between the Green and the Blue

This spectacular house on Ibiza, views over the isle of Es Vedrà included, has the traditional structure of country houses on the islands and at first sight one does not realize that it is new. It was designed and decorated by the owners, the Bosserts. The house has two floors. The ground floor has a beautiful porch with four columns holding up a roof with fragrant savine - red cedar - beams. On the first floor, a balcony with three arches and an iron railing looks out over this magical islet. The white painted walls contrast optimistically with the blue outline of the doors and windows.

Outside, the views over the sea provide a magnificent backdrop for the garden bordered by a stone wall. A table and bench are laid out for open air eating underneath a rustic canopy. An outdoors bathroom has also been installed, shielded off by a staggered wall and decorated by amusing colored ceramic tiles. Having a shower surrounded by such lush natural vegetation can be a pleasure.

Inside, a large living room shares the space with the kitchen and the dining room and a comfortable bedroom. Everything is decorated with exquisite taste, combing the appealing colors of the walls, yellow and lemon green, with the ceramic floor tiles. The furniture is of wood, some of it brightly colored. In the kitchen and bathroom strategically placed tiles create a suggestive melange with a design that never sacrifices comfort nor ease of use.

This cozy corner enjoys a fine view over Es Vedrà. The picturesque canopy is centered over the table of old ceramic tiles. The stone wall has been taken advantage of to form a bench with colorful sky blue cushions playing off against the colors of the table.

Zwischen Grün und Blau

Dieses spektakuläre Hause auf Ibiza mit Blick auf das Eiland Es Vedrà entspricht der typischen ibizenkischen Konstruktionsweise eines Landhauses, wurde jedoch neu gebaut. Für den Entwurf und die Dekoration sind die Eigentümer, das Ehepaar Bossert selbst verantwortlich. Das Haus hat zwei Etagen. Im Erdgeschoss öffnet es sich über eine hübsche Veranda mit vier Pfeilern, die ein Dach aus Zedernholzbalken stützen. Im ersten Stock geben drei mit einem Eisengitter gesicherte Bögen den Blick auf das magische Felseneiland frei. Die Wände sind weiß gestrichen und bilden so einen interessanten Kontrast mit den leuchtend blauen Umrahmungen der Fenster und Türen.

Draußen wird der Platz im Garten, der von kleinen Steinmäuerchen eingefasst ist, genutzt, um einen Essplatz mit Blick aufs Meer einzurichten. Die Sitzbank ist gemauert und der Tisch wird von einer rustikalen Veranda geschützt. Ebenfalls an der frischen Luft wurde eine Dusche vor einer oben unregelmäßig abgestuften Wand, die mit bunten Keramikmosaiken verziert ist, installiert. Unter der üppigen Vegetation kann man die Erfrischung in diesem zauberhaften Umfeld doppelt genießen.

Im Inneren teilen sich das große Wohnzimmer den Raum mit der Küche und dem Esszimmer, während die geräumigen Schlafzimmer an ein komfortables Badezimmer grenzen. Das gesamte Haus ist mit einem exquisiten Geschmack eingerichtet. Die Dekoration stützt sich vor allem auf die Kombination der kräftigen Farben gestrichenen Wände: Gelb und Limonengrün, die sich vom Fußboden aus Tonfliesen absetzen. Die Möbel sind aus Holz und einige wurden mit fröhlichen Tönen gefärbt. In der Küche und im Badezimmer bilden die Einrichtungen mit den mit Bedacht angebrachten Keramikfliesen eine auffällige schöne Kombination, der es weder an Behaglichkeit noch an Komfort fehlt.

Dieser Essplatz vor der Kulisse von Es Vedrà wird von einer rustikalen Veranda überdacht. Der Tisch in der Mitte wurde aus den Resten alter Keramikfliesen selbst gebaut und eine Steinmauer zu einer gemauerten Bank umgestaltet; die Kissen kombinieren Ton in Ton mit den Farben des Tisches.

The house, recently built with local materials adapted to ensure easy living, is traditionally Ibizian in its style. The front patio has a pavement of irregular large stone slabs and is covered by a fantastic porch.

Der Neubau hält sich an die traditionelle ibizenkische Bauweise und wurde mit heimischen Materialien errichtet, die für die gewünschten Zwecke angepasst wurden. Der Boden der Veranda vorne ist mit großen Steinplatten unterschiedlicher Größe ausgelegt.

Outside, next to a well, a rather quaint shower has been installed over the natural rock pavement. Intimacy is provided by the high, staggered wall decorated with an upbeat pattern and, up on a little ledge, dried out starfish. To one side a bench with cushions acts as a complement to the decoration.

Draußen befindet sich in einer Ecke neben einer Zisterne diese einladende Dusche mit einem Boden aus Felsstücken. Die hohe Rückwand ist unregelmäßig abgestuft und wurde mit einem geometrischen Muster in leuchtenden Farben und einem Board, auf dem Seesterne stehen, dekoriert. Gleich daneben steht eine gemauerte Bank mit gemütlichen Kissen und ergänzt das Ensemble.

The kitchen and dining room are in the same space, marked off by a worktop. The different ambiences are defined by the decoration. The lively colors of the cupboard doors, the painted walls, and the classic tiles complement the traditional rustic furniture.

Küche und Esszimmer sind in einem Raum untergebracht, der durch eine Theke und verschiedene Einrichtungselemente begrenzt wird. Die Kombinationen der erfrischenden Farben für einige Schranktüren, die Gestaltung der Wände und ein paar klassische Fliesen werden mit traditionellen und rustikalen Möbeln ergänzt.

The decoration of the bedrooms is based on combining the attractive wall colors with the tulle Thailandes mosquito netting and the bedspreads. The look is refined yet bohemian.

The spacious inside bathroom is brightly lit by the large window, below which sits the bathtub enabling one's gaze to wander outside. The cupboards have sliding doors, painted in an intense blue, and the floor is covered with a raffia mat.

Die Einrichtung der Zimmer des Hauses wird vor allem durch die leuchtenden Farben der Wände bestimmt. Die Moskitonetze aus thailändischem Tüll und die Bettüberwürfe vermitteln eine Bohème-Atmosphäre, die gleichzeitig edel wirkt.

Das Badezimmer im Haus, groß und geräumig, ist von intensiver Helligkeit. In der Badewanne unter dem Fenster kann man sich mit Blick nach draußen entspannen. Die Schränke haben praktische Schiebetüren, die in knalligem Blau gestrichen wurden, und auf dem Boden liegen warme Raphiabast-Matten.

Living by the Sea

Leben am Meer

Living by the Sea

The world is seen in a brighter light on the Pitiusas islands. It is whiter and ideal for photos or filming. Nor do the Edenic qualities end with the light: the islands' crystalline waters are in no way inferior to those of any Caribbean island and therefore Ibiza and Formentera are often used for shooting films or publicity shots. The port of Ibiza has its own magnetic charm and the most romantic way to arrive on the island is by boat, a magical experience. As the ferry comes in one seems to have been transported back in time to another pulsating epoch. The old city, Dalt Vila, declared world heritage by Unesco, rises silently up over the harbor, secure behind it renaissance walls, the harmonious outline of which are impressive. Alley-like, meandering steep streets full of stories and legends whispered on from generation to generation run down to the harbor.

Ibiza and Formentera were one of the center stages for the world hippy movement, when young people were arriving from all round the globe. Not all came just to relax: some wanted to be inspired and many artists and writers hung out here, as well as the finest of the world bohemian class, now long gone. The world has changed since then but this atmosphere still lingers in some places, and some of the characters refused to just fade away.

Maybe they were enchanted by the allure and mysticism of the islands, or enraptured by the sight of the sea off its coasts. Whatever the case, they ended up captivated and so in tune with the peaceful, mellifluous way of life they did not want to uproot and leave. Simple, white rectilinear houses - devoid of any unnecessary ostentation - melt so wonderfully into the landscape that one has to rub one's eyes to check that it is not a mirage. It is the stuff of dreams. Some famous artists could not help writing about what they saw on these islands, people like the learned Luis Salvador Habsburg-Lorena, more commonly known as the archduke Luis Salvador, and others such as Gaspar Melchor de Jovellanos, J. B. Laurens, Santiago Rusiñol and George Sand.

The variety and beauty of the islands is even more exhilarating for mountain lovers. On Mallorca the Tramuntana mountain range has peaks above one thousand meters, offering astonishing views and the most emblematic natural sites. Cliffs are often too savage to allow ports to be formed, but the port of Sòller, Cala Deià, Sa Calobra, and Cala Sant Vicenç stand out. Practically all of this zone, characterized by the abundance of holm oaks, pines and olive trees is protected. The fauna, too, is worthy of note: one inhabitant is the voltor, the black vulture, of which there are few remaining examples in the world.

Leben am Meer

Auf den Pitiusen sieht man die Welt in einem anderen Licht; es ist weißer, ideal zum Fotografieren. Die kristallinen Gewässer stehen denen der Karibikinseln in nichts nach. Aus diesem Grund werden Ibiza und Formentera häufig als Schauplatz für Filmdreharbeiten gewählt. Der Hafen von Ibiza verfügt über eine besondere Anziehungskraft; der schönste Anfahrtsweg ist seit jeher – und wird es für immer sein – vom Meer aus. Es hat etwas Magisches: man wird in eine andere Zeit versetzt und kann die pulsierende Präsenz einer vergangenen Epoche spüren. Die Altstadt, Dalt Vila, von der UNESCO zum Weltkulturerbe erklärt, erhebt sich über der Bucht, beeindruckend in ihrer Stille, wehrhaft hinter ihren Renaissance-Mauern, wunderschön durch die Harmonie ihrer Formen. Ihre engen und steilen Gassen erzählen Geschichten und Legenden, die mündlich weitergegeben werden.

Als Kulisse der Hippie-Bewegung, zu einer Zeit als die Insel weltweit berühmt wurde, kamen Menschen aus allen Ländern der Erde nach Ibiza. Sie war Durchgangsort für Künstler und Schriftsteller, Treffpunkt der distinguiertesten Boheme, die heute verschwunden ist. Diese Ära ist überstanden, aber einige Orte lassen noch das Flair vergangener Zeiten erahnen.

Vielleicht lag es an eben dieser Anziehung, vielleicht am Anblick des Meeres von den Küsten aus – zahlreiche Persönlichkeiten ließen sich von der Lebensart anstecken, vom geheimnisvollen Frieden und der Harmonie, die man hier überall spürt. Die weißen Häuser, einfach und schlicht, ohne jegliche Dekoration, die über das Notwendigste hinausginge, sind derart in die Landschaft eingeflochten, dass man sich die Augen reiben möchte, um sicherzugehen, dass es sich nicht um eine Luftspiegelung handelt. Bekannte Namen haben über die Inseln geschrieben, unter ihnen der Gelehrte Luis Salvador Habsburgo-Lorena, bekannt als Erzherzog Luis Salvador, Gaspar Melchor de Jovellanos, J. B. Laurens, Santiago Rusiñol, George Sand ...

Die Vielfalt und Schönheit der Insel-Landschaften ist für die Liebhaber der Berge grenzenlos. Der Gebirgszug Sierra de Tramuntana auf Mallorca bietet mit seinen über 1.000 Meter aufragenden Gipfeln spektakuläre Panoramablicke und die bekanntesten Natur- und Landschaftsansichten. Die Steilhänge bieten wenig Schutz; von Bedeutung sind daher: die Häfen von Sòller, Cala Deià, Sa Calobra und Cala Sant Vicenç ... Fast das gesamte Gebiet, in dem reichlich Steineichen, Pinien und Olivenbäume wachsen und in dem mehr als 25 heimische Arten und Unterarten vorkommen, ist geschützt. In der Tierwelt sollte man auf den voltor, den schwarzen Geier, achten, von dem es nur noch wenige Exemplare auf der Welt gibt.

RESTAURANTE BAR
7-PM-1-600-92
7-PM-1-173-92
SELVA

Seascapes
Meerlandschaften

Seascapes

Meerlandschaften

The exquisiteness of the landscapes scattered around these islands in the Mediterranean is beyond comparison. Humble words cannot do them justice. Sailing across the surrounding waters you will stumble onto scenes that seem straight out of other worlds, places like Es Vedrà and Na Foradada, from where the archduke Luis Salvador could enjoy divine vistas fit for the god, or breathtaking twilights over Es Grau lagoon.

Lawrence Durrell said one had to reach the islands by sea. Coming in by boat offers the possibility of being welcomed by a towering lighthouse, the sweeping light inviting the traveler to explore the terrain and to enter into the paradise. A good feeling kicks in early.

However, lighthouses are on their way out: the profession of lighthouse keeper is no longer needed, pushed aside by technological advances that will do away with an office that existed one thousand years before Christ when the keepers shone their beams out from strategic points.

A swim among the coral reefs or around the sheer cliffs that drop into the transparent waters is enough to understand why potholers and rock climbers love to come here. Mountaineers can take on the Torrent de Pareis, worth going up just to look down on the stunning scenery. However, if you are after something not quite so tiring there are extensive sandy beaches and delightful little coves hidden away, hewn out of the rocky landscape, some only accessible by boat.

Sailing has many followers on the islands. The Copa del Rey is one of the summer's most prestigious regattas and includes members of the royal family among its participants. Another regatta, unknown to many people, is the Ruta de la Sal - the salt route - which tries to recreate the atmosphere of the sailing boats that took salt, then a valuable commodity, to Barcelona from Ibiza.

Für die Schönheit der Landschaft auf diesen Inseln im Mittelmeer gibt es keinen Vergleich, es fehlen die Worte, sie erschöpfend zu beschreiben. Wer hier segelt wird Zeuge von Szenen aus einer anderen Welt, wie Es Vedrà, oder von himmlischen Meerblicken, die eigentlich den Göttern vorbehalten sind, wie in Na Foradada von den Besitztümern des Erzherzogs Luis Salvador aus, oder eines berauschenden Sonnenuntergangs in der Lagune von Es Grau.

Wenn man vom Meer aus auf die Inseln schaut, empfängt man den Willkommensgruß, den die Gestalt des hohen, blinkenden Leuchtturms in der Dunkelheit aussendet. Es ist eine rhythmische Einladung, sein Territorium kennen zu lernen oder - auch wenn sich nicht alle dessen bewusst sind - ins Paradies einzutreten.

Aber die Tage der Leuchttürme sind gezählt, den Beruf des Leuchtturmwärters gibt es schon nicht mehr. Die Fortschritte der Technik haben dieses alten Gewerbe ersetzt, das bis ins erste Jahrtausend vor Christus zurückreicht und seit jeher auf den Türmen an strategischen Punkten der Küsten ausgeübt wurde.

Nach einem Ausflug zwischen den Riffen und zerfurchten Küsten kann man die Begeisterung der Höhlenforscher verstehen, oder warum es so viele Kletterer hierher zieht. Bergsteiger können sich dem Torrent de Pareis nähern und das Naturschauspiel genießen,

das sich vor ihren Augen ausbreitet. Es gibt aber auch riesige Sandstrände und liebliche, abgeschiedene Buchten.

Segeln gehört zweifellos zu den Sportarten mit den meisten Anhängern auf den Balearen. La Copa del Rey (der Königs-Cup) ist eine der wichtigsten Sommerregatten, und neben vielen anderen nimmt auch die königliche Familie teil. Eine andere, vielen unbekannte Regatta ist die Ruta de la Sal (die Salz-Handelsroute), die mit kleinen Segelbooten (vela latina) die Handelsroute nachfährt, auf der einst ein kostbares Gut, das Salz, von Ibiza nach Barcelona transportiert wurde.

The little isle of Es Vedrà (Ibiza). In the past it was joined to the main isle and with its 385 meter (1 263 feet) sheer vertical walls was the second highest spot on the isle, eclipsed only by S'Atalaia.

Das Felseneiland von Es Vedrà (Ibiza). In der Vergangenheit war es mit der Insel verbunden; mit seinen 385 Meter hohen, fast senkrechten Steilwänden ist es der zweithöchste Punkt der Insel, der nur noch von S'Atalaia übertroffen wird.

Cap de Barberia lighthouse (Formentera).

The principal job of the lighthouse keeper was to keep the beacon shining as the safety of the seafarers depended on it. Often the keeper and their family lived in the lighthouse, well stocked up with non-perishable provisions in case they had to hold out during inclement weather and storms.

Der Leuchtturm vom Cap de Barberia (Formentera).

Der Beruf eines Leuchtturmwärters bestand hauptsächlich darin, das Licht die ganze Nacht hindurch leuchten zu lassen, da die Sicherheit der Seefahrer davon abhing. Oft lebten sie hier mit ihren Familien in totaler Abhängigkeit von den Lebensmittellieferungen von Dritten, die bei Unwetter wesentliche Verzögerungen erleiden konnten.

Botafoch lighthouse (Ibiza)

Der Leuchtturm von Botafoch (Ibiza).

Next page: The lighthouse of the port of Ibiza (photo sup.) The Es Pou lighthouse. (Es Freus is between Ibiza and Formentera) (lower photo)

La Mola lighthouse (Formentera). Most of the lighthouses we can see today were built in the nineteenth century. Now they have fallen into disuse as technology has advanced and this cultural heritage – a symbol of reassurance - is in danger of disappearing.

Auf der folgenden Seite: Der Leuchtturm im Hafen von Ibiza (oben). Der Leuchtturm Es Pou (Es Freus liegt zwischen Ibiza und Formentera) (unten).

Der Leuchtturm von La Mola (Formentera). Die meisten Leuchttürme, die wir heute kennen, wurden im 19. Jahrhundert errichtet. Heute, im Zeitalter des technischen Fortschritts, läuft dieser kulturelle Besitz Gefahr zu verschwinden – und damit auch ein Symbol des sicheren Hafens.

The entrance to the port of Ibiza.

Die schlauchartige Einfahrt in den Hafen von Ibiza.

MIGUEL

Today fishing is no longer one of the mainstays of the local economy. Within the fishing industry small boats, often part of family businesses have pushed aside large-scale fleets. Over 40% of the fish caught is concentrated in the port of Palma, which is followed in importance by the port of Ibiza, and then Cala Figuera and the port of Sóller.

Heute ist der Fischfang für die Wirtschaft der Inseln von geringer Bedeutung; in der Fischerei dominieren die kleinen Boote, oft in Familienbesitz, über große Schiffe. Mehr als 40% des Fischfangs konzentriert sich im Hafen von Palma, danach folgen die Häfen von Ibiza, Cala Figuera und der Hafen von Sóller.

Ibiza port. Fishermen setting out to cast their nets shrouded in the mist. On the islands the fishing is predominated by three species: hake, red mullet and sardine. Other seafood caught includes mollusks like octopus, squid, cuttlefish and crustaceans such as prawns, shrimps, crawfish and lobsters.

Im Morgennebel verlassen die Fischer mit ihren Booten den Hafen von Ibiza, um ihre Netze auszuwerfen. Es gibt verschiedene Arten von Fischen, vorherrschend sind Seehecht, Sardinen und Meerbarben. Der Rest sind Weichtiere wie Kraken, Tintenfische und Sepia sowie Krustentiere wie Garnelen, Kronenhummer und Langusten.

LEVANTE
LEVANTE

AXL. 796

Jetties in Cala Sahona (Formentera). Behind there stand some rudimentary stone constructions where the fishermen keep their tackle.

Ein paar Liegeplätze in der Cala Sahona (Formentera). Im Hintergrund einige primitive Steinbauten, in denen die Fischer ihr Fischereizubehör aufbewahren.

Houses can be this simple and primitive. However, this house gains space by means of a rudimentary wooden porch supported on two trunks and covered by a creeping plant. The dividing line between inside and outside is not clearly defined. The surrounding nature and the possibilities it offers of enhancing a home should never be overlooked.

Die Häuser sind manchmal so primitiv und einfach wie hier, aber der Wohnraum wird oft durch einen Vorbau aus Holz, der auf Stämme gestützt ist und mit einer Kletterpflanze überdacht wird, erweitert. Hier gehen die Grenzen zwischen außen und innen mit Leichtigkeit ineinander über. Die sie einhüllende Natur ist zweifellos ein eindrucksvoller Bestandteil.

Next page:
Islote de S'Espalmador (Formentera). Many sailing boats and motor launches cross daily from Ibiza to Formentera, some of them seduced by the tranquil waters where they may while away the day.

Auf der folgenden Seite: Das Felseneiland von S'Espalmador (Formentera). Viele Segelschiffe und Yachten kreuzen täglich zwischen Ibiza und Formentera. Manche machen auf diesem Felseneiland Halt und genießen seine ruhigen Gewässer.

Page number 276
Portinatx (Ibiza). The rich underwater world means that the islands are an ideal place for practicing scuba-diving and snorkeling.

Seite 276
Portinatx (Ibiza). Die Gewässer um die Inseln sind ideal für den Tauchsport.

Page number 278
There are several legends related to the magnetic field that the beautiful and imposing isle of Es Vedrà is said to generate. One theory is that it forms a magnetic triangle with the rocky outcrop of Ifach (Almería on the Spanish mainland) and the southwest coast of Mallorca, similar to the Bermudas triangle, an area where compasses supposedly no longer work.

Seite 278
Es werden verschiedene Legenden über die magnetische Energie erzählt, die das schöne und eindrucksvolle Felseneiland von Es Vedrà umgibt. Man sagt, dass es mit der Klippe Peñón de Ifach (Almería) und der südwestlichen Küste von Mallorca ein magnetisches Dreieck bildet, das mit dem der Bermudas vergleichbar ist, einem Bereich, in dem der Kompass nicht mehr funktioniert.

Page number 280/281
Es Codolar beach, Ibiza.

Seite 280/281
Der Strand von Es Codolar, Ibiza.

Some of the islands and isles of the Balearic archipelago are protected nature reserves. The archipelago of Cabrera and its surrounding area of sea is the only national park on the Balearic islands. It is considered one of the most precious still-remaining virgin territories in all the Mediterranean. Also, just off the coast by Andratx (Mallorca) lies the nature reserve of Sa Dragonera.

Einige der Inseln und Felseneiländer des balearischen Archipels sind Naturschutzgebiete. Der Archipel von Cabrera und seine Umgebung ist der einzige Nationalpark der Balearen und wird als eine der wertvollsten noch unberührten Gegenden des gesamten Mittelmeers betrachtet. Desgleichen finden wir gegenüber von Andratx (Mallorca) den neuen Naturpark Sa Dragonera.

Outdoor Living: by the Sea

Draussen leben: Am Meer

Outdoor Living: by the Sea

One of the most amazing sights on the islands are the salt plains. The climatic and geomorphologic conditions mean that in these parts of the Mediterranean it is possible to obtain salt by allowing seawater to stagnate. As these areas are protected reserves a great variety of fascinating ecosystems, especially for biologists, are able to thrive, thereby adding the thrill of rare forms of life to the beauty of the scenery. To stroll over these marvelous landscapes contemplating the setting sun subtly changing the colors of the lagoons is an unforgettable spectacle.

On Mallorca you can admire the Salobrar de Campos, and the Colònia de Sant Jordi near to Es Trenc beach, famous for its crystalline, blue waters. L'Albufera (literally the lagoon), an old salt plain on Alcúdia bay is the largest marsh on the islands. It is stocked with fresh water and has the advantage of being a natural park and a protected area for birds. A great attraction for ornithologists, this zone is a natural habitat for over two hundred different species of birds.

On Ibiza salt is produced at Sant Josep de sa Talaia where the union of two islets form the peninsulas of Cap Falcó and Puig del Corb Marí. Very near by there are two sweeping white sandy beaches from where you can see the outline of the island of Formentera and the yachts sailing towards it, sure in the knowledge that they will be able to splash around in the pure waters.

On Formentera, near Estany Pudent, there are two salt producing areas which have fallen into disuse but a great place for a delightful cycling excursion is along the still-remaining channels. This means of transport is very common due to the closeness of everything, and the possibility to marvel at the deliciously wild and peaceful landscapes.

On the beaches the hut-like restaurant are known as chiringuitos. They serve up all types of fried and grilled fish, healthy salads or arròs de peix (fish with rice). Having tried out a genuine regional eating experience you can leisurely digest the food stretched out in the shade of a tree: a siesta is the perfect foil to good food.

Draussen leben: am Meer

Eine der schönsten Landschaften der Balearen findet man in den Salinen. In vielen Dörfern rund ums Mittelmeer wird die Tradition aufrecht erhalten, dank der klimatischen und geomorphologischen Besonderheiten Salz aus der Verdunstung des Meerwassers zu gewinnen. Der Schutz dieser Gegenden, in der mannigfaltige Ökosysteme Platz finden, bewahrt und verstärkt ihre Schönheit bis ins Unendliche. Ein Spaziergang durch diese wunderbaren Landstriche, sich an einem Sonnenuntergang zu erfreuen, zu sehen, wie die Lagunen im wechselnden Licht langsam zu einer wahren Farb-Explosion werden, dies sind unvergessliche Momente.

Auf Mallorca sind Salobrar de Campos und die Colònia de Sant Jordi zugänglich. Sie liegen in der Nähe des Strands Es Trenc, der für den Zauber seines blauen und kristallklaren Wassers berühmt ist. L'Albufera, ein ehemaliges Salzwerk in der Buch von Alcúdia, ist das größte Marschland der Inseln. Es besteht aus Süßwasser und genießt den Vorteil, Naturpark und Vogelschutzgebiet zu sein. Der ornithologische Reichtum ist beeindruckend, denn hier leben mehr als 200 verschiedene Spezies.

Auf Ibiza gibt es Salinen in Sant Josep de sa Talaia, wo sich zwei Felseneilande berühren und die Halbinsel Cap Falcó bilden, sowie Puig del Corb Marí. Ganz in der Nähe liegen zwei weite Strände mit weißem Sand, von denen aus die Silhouette der Insel Formentera und ein paar Segelboote in den Blick kommen, auf der hoffnungsvollen Überfahrt, bald in den idyllischen Gewässern baden zu können.

Auf Formentera um Estany Pudent gibt es zwei Salinen-Gruppen, die nicht mehr in Betrieb sind; es lohnt sich, zwischen ihren Kanälen einen Ausflug mit dem Fahrrad zu machen. Viele Touristen benutzen dank der geringen Größe der Insel dieses Verkehrsmittel. Dadurch kommen sie in den unmittelbaren Genuss einer herrlich unberührten Landschaft, die Natürlichkeit und Ruhe in allen Ecken ausstrahlt.

An den Stränden gibt es eine Vielzahl kleiner Strandbars (chiringuitos), in denen man kleine frische Fische, knackigen Salat oder Reis mit Fisch (arròs de peix) essen kann, um sich später im Schatten eines Baumes auszustrecken und eine herrliche Siesta zu halten.

Previous page:
Porto Colom (Mallorca)

A view of the downtown area around the port of Ibiza. Anchored in the port is one of the ships that connects the island to the mainland and the other islands. Nowadays a catamaran service has cut the journey time down between to Mallorca, Menorca and Formentera.

Auf der vorherigen Seite:
Porto Colom (Mallorca)

Ein Blick auf den Stadtkern von Ibiza, der sich rund um den Hafen schmiegt. Im Hafen ein Schiff, das die Insel mit dem spanischen Festland und den anderen Inseln verbindet. Kürzlich wurde ein Katamaran-Service eingerichtet, der in kurzer Zeit die Entfernungen zwischen den Inseln zurücklegt.

TRASMEDITERRANEA
ALMUDAINA

The city of Ibiza. In the top part you can see the old walled city, Dalt Vila – literally the upper part of the town – and the gothic cathedral of Santa Maria. The old city changed its name several times: for the Carthaginians it was Ibosim, for the Romans it was Ebusus, and for the Arabs either Jebisa or Yabisa, depending on the spelling.

Blick auf die Stadt Ibiza. Oben sind die von einer Mauer umgebene Stadt, Dalt Vila, und die gotische Kathedrale von Santa María zu sehen. Die Altstadt hat mehrere Male ihren Namen gewechselt: für die Karthager hieß sie Ibosim, für die Römer Ebusus, und der in verschiedenen Formen geschriebene arabische Name ist Jebisa oder Yabisa.

DELFIN VERDE
RESTAURANTE
BAR CAN

A view of Porto Colom, in the Felanitx area of Mallorca (upper photo).
The port of Maó (Menorca). There are two cities, Ciutadella and Maó, on this island, located at opposite ends. The character and approach to life of the natives vary depending on which side of the island they come from, but one thing they do have in common, and which is worth remarking on, is their friendly nature and hospitality (lower photo).

Ein Blick auf das Dorf Porto Colom im Gemeindegebiet von Felanitx (Mallorca) (oben). Der Hafen von Maó (Menorca). Auf dieser Insel liegen die beiden Städte, Ciutadella und Maó, an den entgegengesetzten Enden. Der Charakter und die Lebensart der Menorquiner wandelt sich von einem Zipfel der Insel zum anderen; eine Facette ihres liebenswürdigen Charakters muss jedoch hervorgehoben werden: ihre Gastfreundschaft (unten).

Behind the small village of Fornells, on top of a hill, there stands a fantastic tower which protected the settlement and served as a lookout from which to spot approaching enemy boats. For many centuries its was a refuge for the people of the island. Today, as well as being a fine example of the cultural heritage there is a restaurant where you can enjoy a wonderfully flavored lobster caldereta, one of the region's typical dishes (upper photo).

The district of Sa Penya is located next to the entrance to the port of Ibiza (lower photo).

In dem kleinen Dorf Fornells sieht man im Hintergrund auf der Spitze des Hügels einen fantastischen Verteidigungsbau, von dem aus man die Ankunft feindlicher Schiffe beobachten konnte. Jahrhundertelang diente er als Zufluchtsort für die Inselbewohner. Abgesehen von seinem interessanten kulturellen Wert kann man sich dort heute ein sehr schmackhaftes Langustengericht, die caldereta de langosta, eine typische Speise dieser Gegend, schmecken lassen (oben).

Das Stadtviertel von Sa Penya liegt an der schlauchförmigen Hafeneinfahrt von Ibiza (unten).

Views around the island of Mallorca.

El puerto de Sóller (above on the left)

Camp de Mar (above on the right)

A fisherman in front of lighthouse of Alcanada, a small island just off the port of Alcúdia. (below on the left)

Verschiedene Ansichten einiger Orte der Insel Mallorca.

Der Hafen von Sóller (oben links).

Camp de Mar (oben rechts).

Ein Fischer vor dem Leuchtturm von Alcanada, einer kleinen Insel gegenüber dem Hafen von Alcúdia (unten links).

The passion for sailing on the islands is enormous. During the summer prestigious regatas are held and participation is high. The most important is La Copa del Rey (the King's cup) and it never fails to attract the in set who love to be on the scene for this fascinating sport.

Die Begeisterung für den Segelsport auf der Insel ist auffallend. Während des Sommers werden bemerkenswerte Regatten mit großer Beteiligung organisiert. Der Königs-Cup (la Copa del Rey) ist die bedeutendste Regatta; in ihrem Umfeld kann man eine besondere kleine Welt erleben, die dieser faszinierende Sport mit sich bringt.

A great way of getting to know the islands is to sail round their shores. Some people prefer to anchor in one of the pretty inlets, others go to a nearby port, but the majority of boats have a fixed mooring for regular use.

Eine andere Möglichkeit, die Inseln kennenzulernen, ist, ihre Küsten zu umsegeln. Die einen ziehen es vor, in einer der wunderschönen und ruhigen Buchten vor Anker zu gehen, die anderen machen in einem der nahegelegenen Häfen fest; die meisten haben jedoch einen festen Liegeplatz, zu dem sie täglich zurückkehren.

Next pages: The Tramuntana mountain range running along the west of Mallorca offers delightful landscapes that drop down majestic cliffs into the glistening sea.

Auf den folgenden Seiten:
Der Gebirgszug Tramuntana, der sich in Mallorcas Westen von Norden nach Süden erstreckt, bietet mit seinen beeindruckenden Steilküsten, die sich ins Meer stürzen, ein paar der atemberaubendsten Landschaftsansichten.

BAR

The silence and the undisturbed loveliness of this paradise are the keys that make everything fall into perspective for the enchanted beholder.

In der Ruhe und schlichten Schönheit, die dieses Paradies durchdringen, liegt der Schlüssel für eine Begegnung mit dem innersten Selbst.

SUSHAN

The salt producing areas, highly beautiful and biologically interesting, determined the routes of seafarers years back. The conserving properties of salt which enabled perishable foodstuffs to be kept for long periods out on the high seas were an important source of income for Ibiza and Formentera.

Abgesehen davon, dass die Salinen Lebensräume von großer Schönheit und biologischem Reichtum darstellen, legten sie seit Urzeiten die Routen der Seeleute fest. Die konservierenden Eigenschaften des Salzes waren die Lösung für das Überleben auf hoher See während langer Fahrten und ohne frische Verpflegung. Insbesondere für Ibiza und Formentera waren sie eine wichtige Quelle des Reichtums.

Urban areas near the waterfront have been remodernized over the years and charming broadwalks have been built in the most important towns, encouraging the practice of cycling, jogging and roller-skating, all of them against a magnificent backdrop.

Also windsurfers and flysurfers can enjoy the ideal conditions; there are many competitors out on the waves around the islands. Mallorca offers another plus: the local wind called the embat, produced by temperature changes, brings in a sweet breeze at the hottest time of day and puffs out the sails of the boats.

Durch verschiedene städtebauliche Umgestaltungen wurden in den wichtigsten Orten Promenaden entlang der Küste angelegt. Fahrradfahren, Joggen und Rollschuhlaufen sind nur einige der Sportarten, die hier betrieben werden.

Auch die Fans des Windsurfens oder Flysurfens kommen auf ihre Kosten und treffen auf große Konkurrenz. Zu den Besonderheiten der Balearen gehört ein Wind namens embat, der durch die Temperaturschwankungen auf der Insel ausgelöst wird und in den Stunden der stärksten Sonnenstrahlung für eine angenehme Brise sorgt sowie die Segel bläht, für diejenigen, die es aufs Wasser zieht.

MESSENGER
MONTEREY
Inga

The small harbors are excellent places to cool off and freshen up after a day out on the water. There are plenty of friendly watering holes and restaurants with open air terraces where you can feast your eyes on the horizon as you try out the mouth-watering Mediterranean cuisine.

Die kleinen Sporthäfen sind der ideale Rastplatz nach einem Tag auf dem Meer. Hier gibt es nette Kneipen und Restaurants mit Terrassen, auf denen man einige typische Gerichte der Mittelmeerküche genießen kann, ohne die Augen von der Landschaft wenden zu müssen.

RESTAURANTE
Restaurante
La Aventura
PIZZAS

BAR SNACK
MARTINA

The view over Es Cubells bay from the exclusive but welcoming Hotel Las Brisas on Ibiza is impressive.

The swimming pool, just in front of the suites and the hotel's most elegant rooms, is another way of taking in the peacefulness of this part of the island, unaffected by its proximity to the capital. In fact, due to the compactness of the island nothing is too far away.

Vom exklusiven und behaglichen Hotel Las Brisas auf Ibiza kommt man in den Genuss dieses außergewöhnlichen Blicks auf die Bucht Es Cubells.

Der Swimming Pool gegenüber den Suiten und luxuriösen Zimmern des Hotels eignet sich hervorragend, um den Frieden und die Stille zu genießen, die diesen nicht weit von der Hauptstadt (vila) entfernt gelegenen Teil der Insel einhüllt. Tatsächlich ist auf diesem kleinen Eiland alles sehr nah ...

Inside the hotel different zones are decorated in distinct styles. Some features, but not the ceiling which is traditional Ibizian architecture, transport the guest into a totally oriental atmosphere.

Die Inneneinrichtung des Hotels Las Brisas überrascht mit einem Dekorationsstil, der je nach Funktion des Bereiches und andere Atmosphäre kreiert.
Einige Elemente – mit Ausnahme der Decke, da das hölzerne Balkenwerk typisch ist für die traditionelle Inselarchitektur – sollen den Gast in ein orientalisches Ambiente tauchen.

A Cubic Landscape

Situated on a cliff overlooking the glinting blue waters lapping against the island of Formentera, this one storey house is surrounded by a landscape unsurpassable in its beauty. The original project idea was devised and later carried out by one the owners of the house, Miroslav Michalec, together with the architect Christiane Klein. However, the architectural planning and the actual carrying out of the project was handed over to the architects Bill Wright and Ignacio Alonso.

The home, made up of several staggered blocks joined together, advances and recedes, refusing to be tied down to straight lines or simple elevations, but always seeking to maintain the sea's presence through the large windows and rustic porches from which you can gaze out over the horizon.

Inside the combination of distinct ceilings in different zones stands out. Some areas have traditional beams across them while other parts have a flat ceiling and star-shaped openings.

The interior decoration was enthusiastically and lovingly done by the owners, Miroslav and his wife Petra. It is personal, casual and modern, exploiting a mixture of design furniture and other much more traditional, rustic pieces.

In this corner, where there is a set of teak furniture, you can appreciate the differences in the house structures and the rough and smooth finishes of the walls, though all of them have in common the color ochre.

Würfel-Landschaft

Auf einer Klippe über dem Meer mit seinen blauen und kristallklaren Gewässern, die die Insel Formentera umspülen, erstreckt sich dieses Haus mit nur einem Geschoss, umgeben von einer einzigartigen Landschaft.

Die Idee für dieses Haus stammt vom Eigentümer selbst, Miroslav Michalec und der Architektin Christiane Klein, die beide auch die Ausführung übernommen haben. Für die detaillierte architektonische Planung und formale Abwicklung sind die Architekten Bill Wright und Ignacio Alonso verantwortlich.

Das Ensemble, das aus mehreren aufgereihten würfelförmigen Elementen besteht, springt vor und zurück, um eine lineare Anordnung des Grundrisses und Schnitts zu vermeiden und sucht zugleich durch großflächige Fenster und rustikale Veranden zum Wasser hin eine Annäherung an das Meer.

Drinnen fällt besonders die Kombination der in den einzelnen Bereichen unterschiedlichen Gestaltung der Decken auf: die einen im traditionellen Stil mit Holzbalken, die anderen glatt verputzt.

Die Inneneinrichtung wurde mit viel Liebe und Enthusiasmus von den Besitzern, Miroslav und seiner Frau Petra, gestaltet. Sie verkörpert einen sehr persönlichen, modernen und informellen Stil, der Designerstücke mit rustikalen Möbeln mischt.

In dieser Ecke, in der Teakholz-Möbel angeordnet wurden, kann man die Größenunterschiede der verschiedenen Abschnitte des Hauses sowie die unterschiedliche Gestaltung der Wände erkennen. Sie werden durch die Ocker-Farbe, in die das gesamte Ensemble getaucht ist, vereinheitlicht.

The east-facing house façade with its porches offering fantastic vistas over the sea.

Die Ostseite des Hauses öffnet sich über mehrere Veranden zu diesem traumhaften Blick auf das Meer.

The west-facing façade runs down three steps to the façade overlooking the sea. Notice how the total surface area of the walls is thus reduced.

Die Fassade der Westseite fällt über drei Abstufungen zum Meer hin ab; so wurde die Gesamtoberfläche der Wände reduziert.

This corner shows how the walls take advantage of contrast and composition in the finishes. Smoothness is played off against roughness, another small detail to give a definitive touch.

An dieser Ecke wird sichtbar, wie die Verarbeitung der Mauern mit dem Kontrast und der Komposition des Ensembles spielt: glatte Wände wechseln sich mit rauen ab. Diese kleinen Details geben dem Entwurf den letzten Schliff.

The two façades of the houses run into one another. One can move around depending where the sun is: in winter you can seek out its warm rays and in summer it is cooler in the shade.

In the outdoor paving there are small pebbles set into the ground to mark off some zones such as the steps, or simply for discrete straight-lined decoration.

Next page:
Solid, uncompromising wood, used for the dining room and the kitchen, provides a warm and comfortable feeling. Star-shaped openings in the ceilings are an original way of providing natural daylight for the room, and give a dynamic twist to the decoration.

Der Durchgang verbindet die beiden Seiten des Hauses miteinander und ermöglicht es, sein Plätzchen je nach dem Stand der Sonne zu wählen: im Winter zur Sonne hin, im Sommer vor ihr flüchtend.

Im Bodenbelag der Außenbereiche kann man kleine runde Kiesel erkennen, die einige Bereiche, wie die Treppenstufen, abgrenzen oder einfach den Boden durch kleine durchgängige Linien verschönern.

Auf der folgenden Seite: Das Holz, solide und schnörkellos, das für das Esszimmer und die Küche ausgewählt wurde, gibt dem Raum eine warme und komfortable Note.
Für den Einfall natürlichen Lichts wurde in einigen Zimmern ein originelles System gewählt: Sternformen in der Decke schmücken den Raum und verleihen ihm zugleich Dynamik.

The variations in the ceilings change the mood significantly as one goes around the home. Another factor in creating the ambience are the chimney designs. The singular ceiling – the star-shaped light reflected off the floor has already been seen in the kitchen – opens up the possibility of some very original variations in the decoration.

Die unterschiedlichen Gestaltungsweisen der Decke stellen wesentliche Veränderungen des Ambientes dar. Das Design der Kamine lässt sie ebenfalls eine wichtige Rolle für die Atmosphäre spielen. Das Deckendetail der Sterne, das man schon in der Küche gesehen hat, spiegelt sich auf dem Boden wider und sorgt für interessante Effekte.

Within the bedroom there is a bathroom hidden away behind a half-height wall.

The highly personal toilet design is just right for spaces where there is not an inch to spare.

Das Bad ist im Schlafzimmer integriert und wird nur durch eine halbhohe Mauer abgeteilt.

Die sehr persönliche Gestaltung des Waschbeckens ist für einen so kleinen Raum ideal.

Feet in the Water

Sometimes the element of surprise plays a key role in architecture, especially at a time when brilliance and creativity are noticeable for their absence. Therefore it is even more rewarding to come across projects like this one by the innovative Josep Lluís Mateo of MAP Arquitectes. At the Colònia de Sant Pere, near Artà on Mallorca, he has carefully designed a residence taking full advantage of the surrounding natural blessings by the sea. The architect himself also took on the interior design.

The original structure is due to architect's intention to combine creativity and ingenuity and ensure that although north facing - the view was too tempting to turn one's back on - the building would be protected from the tramuntana wind coming from the north. Another important objective was to channel the light coming from the south-side towards the living quarters with their magnificent vistas. The solution was to use glass heavily on the ground floor - the building tends towards transparency - and windbreaks which restrain the wind's force. The patios make outside areas liveable thus increasing the house's useful space.

The compositional esence of the house is defined by two parallelepiped volumes, one intense blue and the other white, running into each other perpendicularly to form a T. The interplay between the contrasting colors is an attempt to blend in with the sea and the sky, and to break the cubic compositional coldness of the façade.

The home is divided up into three stories, including the underground garage which exploits the slope of the land. On the ground floor there is the living room, the outdoor summer dining room, the winter dining room and the kitchen. On the top floor there are three bedrooms, a guest room and a small studio. In some ways the inside of the house is reminiscent of a boat. The decoration is modern yet functional.

The great natural beauty of the house's setting with its view over the Llevant mountain range is undeniable. The combination of diverse materials on the side façade is visible in this photo: black painted steel shielding off the garage ramp, the darkened wood of the door, the marés stonework with square openings, and the blue and white concrete are strikingly attractive together.

One of the house's several patios, shielded by the windbreaks, leads into the guest room. The nautical staircase here adds an original touch (left).

Die Füsse im Wasser

Es kommt vor, dass die Überraschung eine fundamentale Rolle in der Architektur spielt. So entstand in einem Winkel der Insel Mallorca, in der Colònia de Sant Pere (Artà), dieses verspielte und persönliche Wohnhaus, in bester Lage direkt am Meer. Es ist ein avantgardistischer Entwurf von Josep Lluís Mateo, MAP Arquitectes; der ebenfalls für die Gestaltung der Innenräume verantwortlich ist.

Der ungewöhnliche Aufbau ist das Ergebnis des Zusammenspiels von Kreativität und Einfallsreichtum, wodurch überzeugende Lösungen für die beiden schwachen Stellen des Projektes gefunden wurden: die Nord-Orientierung, um die Aussicht aufs Meer genießen zu können, und die Notwendigkeit, das Haus vor dem starken Tramuntana-Nordwind zu schützen.

Außerdem war es wichtig, das Licht der Südseite durch den Wohnbereich zu lenken, da die spektakuläre Aussicht eben gerade auf der anderen, der Nord-Seite liegt. Dieses Ziel wurde einerseits dadurch erreicht, dass man das Erdgeschoss in Nord-Süd-Richtung großflächig verglaste und andererseits mehrere Innenhöfe (patios) und Wandscheiben die Kraft des Windes brechen. Die patios vergrößern zudem die Wohnfläche nach draußen.

Das Gebäude besteht aus mehreren Baukörper mit verschiedenen Einschnitten, die Einblick in die innere Aufteilung geben. Im Prinzip wird die Komposition durch zwei Hauptkörper definiert, die quasi ineinander gesteckt wurden. Sie unterscheiden sich durch ihre weiße und knallblaue Farbe und bilden ein T.

Das kontrastreiche Farbspiel passt sich der umgebenden Natur, dem Himmel und dem Meer an und lockert außerdem die eckige und eher kalte Anordnung der Fassade auf.

Die Wohnung erstreckt sich über drei Geschosse, denn das Gefälle des Geländes wurde genutzt, um die Garage unter die Erde zu verlegen. Darüber, im Erdgeschoss, ordnen sich das Wohnzimmer, die Sommer- und Winter-Essplätze sowie die Küche an. In der oberen Etage wurden drei Schlaf-, ein Gäste- und ein kleines Arbeitszimmer eingerichtet. Die Dekoration ist modern, praktisch und funktionell.

Die Lage dieses Hauses, von dem man diesen unvergleichlichen Blick auf den Gebirgszug Serra de Llevant hat, ist wirklich beneidenswert. Für die seitliche Fassade wurden verschiedene Materialien kombiniert: schwarz gestrichener Stahl, der das Grundstück und die Rampe der Garagenzufahrt begrenzt, dunkel gewordenes Holz für die Tür, eine Mauer mit kleinen Öffnungen aus dem Kalkstein marès und blau und weiß gestrichener Beton – alles zusammen wirkt auffällig und attraktiv.

Einer der vielen patios (Innenhöfe) des Hauses, geschützt zwischen Mauern gelegen, führt in das Gästezimmer. Die Treppe, die auch auf ein Schiff passen würde, ist in diesem Zusammenhang sehr originell (links).

The outdoor summer dining room is protected from the Tramuntana wind by the wall of marés stone. However, the openings let sunlight through.

Stairs lead up to the main entrance on the northern façade.

Der Sommer-Essplatz liegt geschützt hinter dieser Mauer aus marès mit quadratischen Durchbrüchen, die das Sonnenlicht durchlässt und vor dem Tramuntana-Wind schützt; außerdem ist er mit Rohrgeflecht gedeckt.

Eine Treppe überwindet die Höhenunterschiede des Geländes und bildet den Zugang zum Haupteingang an der Nordseite.

The northwesterly façade highlights the contrast between the white and the blue. The second volume, overtly Mediterranean, reflects the intense blue of the sky and the sea, in constant dialogue with surrounding nature, ensuring that the building softly blends in with the landscape (above).

The south façade receives warmth and light all day. The lawn and deckchairs help to put you in a frame of mind for relaxing. The openings in the walls were conceived to guarantee views of the sea from one end of the house to the other (below).

Die nördliche Fassade zeigt deutlich die Verschachtelung der beiden Gebäudekörper in ihrem weiß-blauen Kontrast. Der blaue Teil, durch und durch mediterran, spielt mit den intensiven Farbtönen des Himmels und des Meeres und steht in einem unablässigen Dialog mit der umgebenden Landschaft, während er gleichzeitig die Präsenz des Gebäudes mildert (oben).

Die nach Süden ausgerichtete Fassade nimmt während des Tages das Licht und die Wärme der Sonne auf. Die Rasenfläche und die bequemen Liegen tragen dazu bei, dass eine entspannte und ruhige Atmosphäre entsteht. Der Architekt gestaltete die Mauern von einer Seite des Hauses zur anderen transparent, um von allen Punkten des Hauses den Blick auf das Wasser genießen zu können (unten).

In the foreground we can see the inner dining room with its modern, practical decoration. In the background is the living room, decorated according to the same guidelines, from where one can look out over the expanse of sea.

Im Vordergrund sieht man das Esszimmer drinnen mit seiner modernen und funktionalen Einrichtung. Im Wohnzimmer dahinter wird der gleiche Dekorationsstil beibehalten; von hier hat man Blick auf das offene Meer.

The master bedroom, facing north in the white block – what could be considered as the prow of the boat – has the best view of Cape Ferrutx. The white painted wood shutters gracefully blend in with the external façade. The suite bathroom of the master bedroom.

Das Elternschlafzimmer, im 'Schiffsbug' bzw. der nach Norden blickenden Fassade (im weißen Baukörper) gelegen, hat den besten Panoramablick über das Kap Ferrutx. Einige der Fensterläden sind aus Holz und zum Schieben, andere haben ein Scharnier; sie sind weiß gestrichen und in die Fassade integriert. Das modern gestaltete Badezimmer ist direkt mit dem Schlafzimmer verbunden.

Walls are scarce in the kitchen as sliding glass doors communicate directly with the interior dining room on the right, the outdoor summer dining room and one of the patios, and beyond the garden. This practical and original arrangement means that, flying in the face of convention, the worktable and sink have been placed in the middle and not against the walls.

Die Küche hat nur eine einzige Wand, da sie über gläserne Schiebtüren mit dem rechts von ihr liegenden Esszimmer, mit dem Sommer-Essplatz in einem der Innenhöfe davor und mit dem Garten verbunden ist. Dieses sowohl praktische als auch originelle Design machte es erforderlich, die Arbeitsfläche mit der Spüle in der Mitte des Raumes anzuordnen und nicht wie in den meisten Fällen entlang einer Wand.

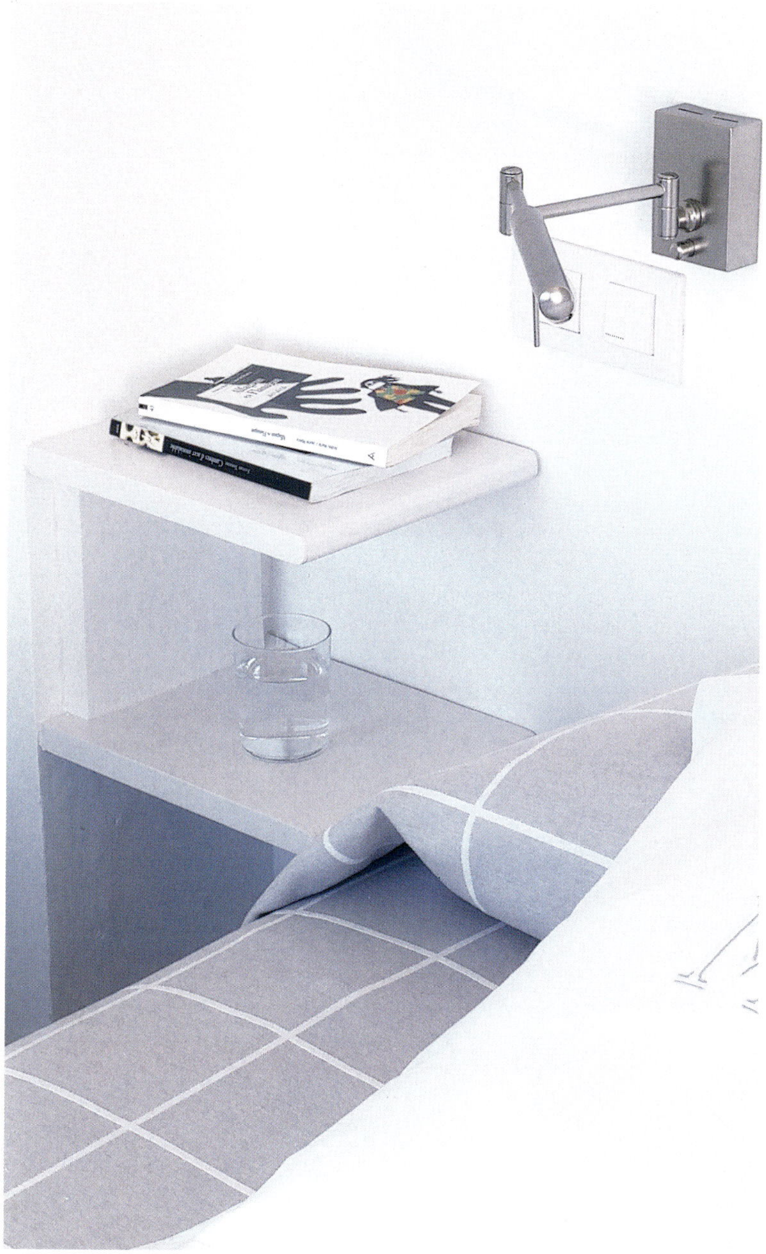

The staircase running up to the bedrooms on the first floor brings to mind the interior design of a boat.

Die Treppe in die erste Etage, in der sich die Schlafzimmer befinden, erinnert mit ihrem Design an das Innere eines Schiffes.

A Fortress Reincarnated

On the gorgeous bay of Pollença, in the northeast of Mallorca, an old military fort, known as El Castell, was converted into a private home in 1927. Recently, the B&B&W Estudio de Arquitectura, Sergi Bastides and Wolf Siegfried Wagner, was given the remit of converting El Castell de Sant Pere into a modern home. Peter Preller of Hamburg designed the interiors.

The project had to comply with the "Law of the National Heritage of the Balearics Islands" as the fort is of cultural interest. The home, in the middle of a landscape so beautiful you have to check you are not dreaming, is surrounded by a moat, used in the old days for the water supply. In front of the building, the esplanade stretches out towards the mounds on which the canons were placed, facing out over the sea.

The converted fort has two floors and a roof sloping down on two sides. The primitive external structure and the neat façade were respected, and the windows and doors were left unchanged, thus it still gives the sensation of being a stronghold. The rear façade is the only part of the building that was not modified.

The principal entrance façade was given the look of a little Italian palace out of the renaissance period, characterized by the solemnity of its lines and the symmetry of the façade.

The fort is set overlooking a generous esplanade. Beyond lies the sea. There are some chairs for lounging in and for looking out over the bay. The entrance to the site goes up three steps. Inside the fort, Preller came up with modern, elegant and luxurious living quarters, in certain zones not being afraid to go for the latest designs as evidenced by the kitchen and bathroom.

The old entrance passes between the walls, marking off the elevation of the fort and offering protection. The rear façade was left unchanged – the ground floor decorated by the stonework. On the upper floor the façade was integrated with the rest of the building, reformed in 1927. On the little balcony, where in the previous reform marès stonework had been used, a stainless steel railing was fitted. As it is visually low-key, the building's military aspect is emphasized. The main façade stands out against the bay of Pollença, a fine testimony to the unparalleled beauty of the north of the island.

Eine wiederbelebte Festung

In der wunderschönen Bucht von Pollença im Nordosten der Insel Mallorca, steht die alte militärische Festung El Castell, die bereits seit 1927 als Privathaus genutzt wird. Das Architekturbüro B&B&W Estudio de Arquitectura, Sergi Bastides und Wolf Siegfried Wagner setzten einen Architekturentwurf um, der die alte Festung von Sant Pere in ein modernes Wohnhaus verwandelte. Die innenarchitektonische Gestaltung stammt von Peter Preller (Hamburg).

Das Projekt muss den Anforderungen des Denkmalschutzgesetzes der Balearen genügen, da es sich um ein Bauwerk von allgemeinem kulturellen Interesse handelt. Es befindet sich in einer paradiesischen Landschaft und hat Zugang zu einem kleinen Sandstrand. Der Festungsgraben, der es umgibt, wurde als Sammelbrunnen genutzt. Zum Wasser hin liegt die ehemalige Befestigunglage zur Verteidigung, auf der fünf Kanonen in Position standen.

Das Haus hat zwei Geschosse sowie ein flaches Giebeldach. Die äußere einfache Struktur und ihre authentischen Öffnungen wurden beibehalten, so dass in der schnörkellosen Fassade keine Veränderungen auszumachen sind. Auf diese Weise bewahrt das Haus das Aussehen einer Festung, vor allem an der rückwärtigen Fassade, die einzige, die völlig intakt war.

Die Frontseite mit dem Haupteingang sollte das Aussehen eines italienische Palazzo aus der Renaissance bekommen, ausgedrückt durch die durchweg schlichte Linienführung und die Symmetrie der Fassade.

Das Gebäude erhebt sich über einer Terrasse, auf der Bänke aufgestellt wurden, um den fantastischen Blick auf die Bucht genießen zu können. Vor dem Eingang befindet sich ein Garten, zu dem man über drei Stufen gelangt, die den Höhenunterschied ausgleichen. Im Inneren verbirgt sich eine moderne Wohnung, die nach den Ideen von Peter Preller gestaltet wurde. Die Einrichtung ist elegant und in einigen Bereichen wie der Küche oder dem Bad avantgardistisch.

Der alte Zugangsweg verläuft nach wie vor zwischen den Mauern, die seine erhöhte Lage gegenüber dem Grundstück unterstreichen. An der hinteren Fassade ist im ersten Stock noch die Wand aus Quadersteinen intakt. Die Außenstruktur der oberen Etage, bereits 1927 renoviert, wurde den restlichen Fassaden angeglichen. Das frühere Geländer aus Marès-Stein (von der ersten Renovierung) wurde durch ein neues aus sandgestrahltem Stahl ersetzt, das unauffälliger ist und das Aussehen der Festung nicht beeinträchtigt. Die Frontseite hebt sich vor der Bucht von Pollença ab, die für die einmalige Schönheit des Nordens dieser Insel steht.

The entrance hall has a double-height ceiling. A staircase with a stainless steel and glass banister leads up to the first floor where the large windows let in abundant light ensuring that even the ground floor is luminous. The light tones of the decoration and the Santanyí stone pavement adds to the spacious feeling all over the ground floor.

Der Hauseingang öffnet sich zu einem Raum mit doppelter Raumhöhe, von dem eine Treppe mit einem Geländer aus sandgestrahltem Edelstahl und Glas die obere Ebene erschließt. Licht strömt über breite Fenster ins Wohnzimmer. Die Einrichtung in hellen Tönen auf dem Steinboden aus der mallorquinischen Stadt Santanyí vergrößert diesen Raum, der tatsächlich das ganze Erdgeschoss einnimmt.

The modern kitchen design combines stainless steel, common in the catering trade, with a wood colored worktop which softens the coldness of the metal. The translucent glass of the cupboards and the glass of the cooking hood are perfect complements for this pleasant, brightly lit kitchen.

Für die Küche wurde ein modernes Design ausgewählt, das Edelstahl, das normalerweise in Großküchen eingesetzt wird, mit einer Arbeitsfläche in einem Holzton kombiniert, wodurch die Kälte des Metalls aufgewogen wird. Die originellen Schränke haben Türen aus Mattglas und die Dunstabzugshaube eine Hülle aus transparentem Glas. Sie ergänzen das freundliche und helle Aussehen der Küche.

In the bedroom Preller stuck to his intention to decorate the house discretely, always aiming at subtle elegance. Only the bold color of the armchair and the pillows on the bed contrast with the cream tone of the rest of the room.

Das Schlafzimmer ist in der diskreten und zarten Eleganz gehalten, die für den Einrichtungsstil Prellers charakteristisch ist. Der Crèmeton wird nur durch den Sessel unter dem Fenster unterbrochen, der zu den Kissen auf dem Bett passt.

The wood beams of the ceiling match the tone of the walls, an ideal backdrop for this contemporary bathroom design. The flooring is of wood varnished white. The very select designer Philippe Starck created the modern bath and all the units were supplied by the company Aqua Aquae.

Unter einer Decke aus Holzbalken, Ton in Ton mit den Wänden, präsentiert sich das Badezimmer mit seinem Fußboden aus weiß beschichteten Holz in einem avantgardistischen Design. Die Badewanne ist ein Entwurf des Designers Philippe Starck. Die gesamte Einrichtung wurde von der Firma Aqua Aquae geliefert.

The setting of the house, raised up over the surrounding land and looking over the sea, next to a sandy bay, is a gift from nature. The impressive panoramic view of the coast of Mallorca shows the advantageous position of the fort and the visibility it enjoyed, unbeatable for defending the town from enemy incursions. Canons stood between the battlements on the edge of the esplanade, but now peace reigns and harmony with the natural surroundings means that the only option is to relax totally and lie down under the Mediterranean sun.

Die Lage des Hauses auf der Landzunge und neben einer kleinen Bucht mit Sandstrand ist wirklich ein unübertreffliches Geschenk. Das beeindruckende Panorama der Küste Mallorcas lässt hier deutlich die Lage und Aussicht der Festung erkennen, die von hier die Küste gegen fremde Eindringlinge verteidigt hat. Auf der alten Esplanade standen mehrere Kanonen zwischen den Zinnen. In Zeiten des Friedens und in Harmonie mit der Umgebung bleibt nur noch, sich in der Sonne des Mittelmeers zu baden und völlig entspannt auf den Liegen auszuruhen.

A Small Dose of Heaven

This nigh on one hundred year old farmhouse on Cala Llombarts, Mallorca, very near to Santanyí, is in an area covered by pine trees. Once again the views over the sea provide no rest for the eye. The owner is a descendent of an old Majorcan family that used to work the land and breed livestock not too many decades back. His grandson, Antoni Muntaner, reformed the house and stables and converted them into a modern home. The interior design project was also under his charge. Now, sometimes he himself lives in the house; on occasions he lends it out to friends and during other seasons he rents it out.

Access to the house is along a rough and winding track, not perfect but better than before. The terrain of the house is extended by terracing on two levels which runs to the very edge of the rocks and offers marvelous vistas over the waters.

Inside the house, the original structure has been left almost untouched. The wooden rafters are still painted white and the floor is covered with handmade ceramic tiles. A partition and shelving divides the living space. An archway leads to the master bedroom. The other bedrooms are part of the old stable conversion where the horses were kept and the hay stored, called pallisa in the Majorcan language.

The decoration and the furniture, chosen by the owner himself, are a personal mix of traditional Majorcan elements and importations from Morocco.

The panoramic view from this terrace, shaded by a robust pine tree, is livened up by the glittering dancing reflections off the sea, which go from emerald green through to the deepest blue. On the terrace there is a Moroccan rug, a few Turkish cushions and a ceramic lamp by Stanislas Carrelet. It is one of the loveliest places imaginable for reading or merely contemplating nature.

Eine Prise Himmel

In der Cala Llombarts (Mallorca), ganz in der Nähe von Santanyí, liegt dieses kleine, fast 100 Jahre alte Landhaus mitten in einem Pinienwald und mit berauschender Aussicht aufs Meer. Der Eigentümer gehört zu einer alten mallorquinischen Familie, die sich vor nicht allzu Zeit der Landwirtschaft und Viehzucht widmete. Sein Enkel, Antoni Muntaner, renovierte das Haus und richtete die bestehende Wohnung ein. Für Innenausbau und Dekoration zeichnet auch er verantwortlich. Momentan nutzt er die Wohnung nur sporadisch, überlässt sie oft Freunden oder vermietet sie von Zeit zu Zeit.

Über einen etwas holprigen und verschlungenen Weg, der vorsichtig nachgebessert wurde, gelangt man zu dem Häuschen. Draußen wurde der Wohnraum um zwei Terrassenebenen verlängert, die bis an die Steilküste reichen und traumhafte Meerblicke bieten.

Der alte Innenaufbau des Hauses ist fast intakt: Die alten Holzbalken wurden weiß gestrichen, der Fußboden mit handgefertigten Tonziegeln ausgelegt und das Wohnzimmer durch eine eingezogene Wand geteilt, in der ein Regal eingebaut ist. Ein lustiger spitzer Bogen führt durch diese Trennwand ins größte Schlafzimmer. Die anderen Zimmer wurden im ehemaligen Stall und in der Scheune eingerichtet

Die Dekoration und das Mobiliar wurden vom Eigentümer ausgesucht und stellen eine sehr persönliche Mischung dar, die irgendwo zwischen der mallorquinischen und der marokkanischen Kultur angesiedelt ist.

Wenn man von dieser Terrasse im Schatten einer alten Pinie aufs Meer blickt, zaubert das Wasser nach seinem Gutdünken spiegelnde Reflexe, die von Smaragdgrün bis ins tiefste Ozeanblau reichen. Auf dem Boden wurde ein marokkanischer Teppich, einige türkische Kissen und eine Keramiklampe von Stanislas Carrelet arrangiert, so dass man sich nur noch niederlassen und lesen oder die Natur betrachten möchte.

The Hitch Hiker's Guide to the Galaxy
DOUGLAS ADAMS

The entrance porch has stone pillars and is covered by white canvas. Once again the view will draw a few gasps. Some leaning pines bring to mind a raging storm, even though they are not very common on these islands.

Die Eingangsveranda, zwischen deren Steinsäulen ein weißes Segeltuch-Dach gespannt ist, liegt auf einem Vorsprung, der einem diese fantastische Aussicht beschert. Ein paar schiefe Pinien erinnern an die Kraft der letzten Stürme, die in diesem Landstrich ansonsten sehr selten sind.

On the main façade of the house the old marés stone walls – much more resistant than modern materials – can still be seen. The glass door, visible in the photo, allows daylight in. The other door, made of wood, leads into the house. The rug, the lamp and the table are all from Morocco.

An der Front des Hauses sieht man den alten Marès-Stein, der viel robuster ist, als der, den man heute verwendet. Der Eingang hat eine verglaste Doppeltür, die das Tageslicht durchlässt, und eine Holztür, die sich ins Haus hinein öffnet. Der Teppich, die Lampe und der Tisch stammen aus Marokko.

Inside the house, the master bedroom was separated off from the living room by this shelving which fits in beneath the slope of the ceiling. With a wink at oriental design, there is an ogee arched opening in the middle.

Drinnen wurde das Schlafzimmer mittels dieses gemauerten Regals vom Wohnzimmer getrennt. Es passt sich der Dachschräge an und öffnet in der Mitte einen Durchgang mit einem orientalisch angehauchten Bogen.

Some fittings around the house are typical of life in the country on Mallorca: the cistern, the chimney around which the families used to cook and gather, and this vintage table made of wood. Neither does the picture of "Sitting Bull" go unnoticed.

Im Wohnzimmer sieht man die typische Ausstattung eines mallorquinischen Landhauses und seine traditionellen Elemente: der Brunnen im Inneren des Hauses, der Kamin zum Kochen und um den sich das Leben abspielte und ein alter Holztisch. Darauf steht ein gerahmtes Bild des legendären Sitting Bull.

TATANKA YOTANKA
SITTING BULL

A House with a View

This house on Ibiza looks out over the sea and the gorgeous countryside. It has its own swimming pool set in an ample terrace going down to the porch. Inside, the home is spacious and comfortable. The designer Lorenzo Queipo del Llano conceived the furniture. The first of the porches, supported by four solid pillars, is of wood and runs into another much more rustic one covered by a creeping plant.

Moving inside, the sizable living room plays with the different floor and ceiling levels. In the house design the priorities were always comfort and openness. The kitchen is marked off by a step and a doorway. The simplicity of the shelving and the glass cupboards, contrasting provocatively with the dark wood, perfectly integrate the cooking space.

The master bedroom is on the first floor and opens up to the exterior accessing onto two terraces. The more traditional one has several arches while the other, bigger and covered by reeds, offers great views over the garden and, beyond, the sea.

The couch, the hammock under the porch and natural surroundings that seem to suggest paradise can be reached a give off a calmness that seems from another world, an island stillness.

Ein Haus mit Aussicht

Dieses Haus auf Ibiza mit Blick auf Meer und umgebendes Land hat ein Schwimmbad und großzügige Terrassen, die auf die Veranda hinunterführen. Das Ambiente in den Innenräumen ist weitläufig und komfortabel. Die Möbel wurden von dem Designer Lorenzo Queipo del Llano entworfen. Die Veranda öffnet sich nach draußen über eine, von vier riesigen Pfeilern getragene Holzdecke, die durch einen weiteren, rustikaleren verlängert wird und mit einer Kletterpflanze gedeckt ist.

Innen nimmt das Wohnzimmer einen weitläufigen Raum ein, der mit mehreren Niveauunterschieden und verschiedenen Höhen mit der bequemen und offenen Struktur des Hauses spielt. In die Küche gelangt man über einen kleinen Absatz durch ein Bogenportal. Regale aus Mauerwerk und verglaste Wandschränke, die einen attraktiven Kontrast zu dem dunklen Holz bilden, schaffen eine angenehme Atmosphäre.

Im ersten Stockwerk liegt das große Schlafzimmer, das sich über zwei Terrassen nach draußen öffnet. Eine davon, mit mehreren Bögen, ist traditioneller gehalten, während die andere weitläufiger und mit Rohrgeflecht abgedeckt ist, aber beide geben den Blick auf Meer und Garten frei.

Der Diwan, die Hängematte unter der Veranda und die anregende natürliche Umgebung sind der Rahmen einer Atmosphäre voller Gelassenheit und Entspannung auf den Inseln der Ruhe.

THE AUTHORS WISH TO THANK
DIE AUTOREN DANKEN

Special thanks to the house owners, for their kindness and willingness to let us into the privacy of their own homes.
Ganz besonders danken wir den Eigentümern der Häuser für ihre Liebenswürdigkeit, uns Zutritt zu ihren Wohnungen zu gewähren.

To the professionals who have realised or participated in the architectural and interior design projects.
Den Architekten und Innenarchitekten, die die Entwürfe umgesetzt oder daran mitgewirkt haben.

To our families, with love, for their patience and understanding
Von Herzen unseren Familien für ihre Geduld und ihr Verständnis.

As well as to the following persons and institutions:
Sowie den folgenden Personen und Institutionen:

The Skipper of Llevant, Toni.
Dem Skipper der Llevant, Toni.
Anick & Jean Ferré
Antonio Muntaner, *Santanyí* (Mallorca)
Aqua-Aquae, *Manacor* (Mallorca)
Bordados Joana Villalonga, *Porto Cristo* (Mallorca)
Centre de Cultura Sa Nostra, Albert Ribas, *Palma* (Mallorca)
Cerámicas Stanislas Carrelet, *Cas Concos* (Mallorca)
Coconut Company, *Manacor* (Mallorca)
Cristina & José Luis, El Chiringuito, *Es Cavallet* (Ibiza)
Denario Sa Tenda, *Palma* (Mallorca)
Fundació Pilar i Joan Miró, *Palma* (Mallorca)
Hotel Las Brisas (Renée & Manu), *Puig Roig* (Ibiza)
Hotel Les Terrasses (Ibiza)
Hotel Son Gener, *Son Servera* (Mallorca)
Ino Coll
Joan des Pou
Lorenzina (Decoration/Dekoration), *Ca na Negreta* (Ibiza)
Luís Rodríguez Mori
Maison de l'Elephant, Bruno Reymond (Ibiza)
Menestralia, (Glass craftmanship/Glas-Kunsthandwerk) (Mallorca)
Pastelería Sucrart, *Port de Pollença* (Mallorca)
Pinu Albanese, Cerámicas Hellas, *Can Bellotera* (Ibiza)
Rafael Calparsoro & Marlene Alvadalejo
Rafaël Pialoux
Restaurante Colón, *Porto Colom* (Mallorca)
Ricardo Urgell
Restaurante El Ayoun, *Sant Rafael* (Ibiza)
Scott's Hotel, *Binissalem* (Mallorca)
Unicorn (Interior Design/Inneneinrichtung), Nona von Haeften, *Manacor* (Mallorca)
Vidrieras Gordiola, *Algaida* & *Palma* (Mallorca)

Special Contributions:
Besondere Mitwirkung:
Stylist
Stylist
Elena Calderón (Restored Tradition/Bewahrte Tradition, Between Green and Blue/Zwischen Grün und Blau, A House with a View/Ein Haus mit Aussicht, Hotel Las Brisas).

Tourist information
Touristeninformation

Oficina d'Informació i Turisme
Avinguda Jaume III, 10
07012 Palma de Mallorca, (Balears), España
☎ +34-971 71 22 16

Oficina d'Informació i Turisme
C/ Antoni Riquer, 2
07800 Eivissa (Ibiza) (Balears), España
☎ +34-971 30 19 00

Oficina d'Informació i Turisme
C/ Sa Rovellada de Dalt, 24
07730 Maó, (Balears), España
☎ +34-971 36 37 90